ENHANCING INTIMACY IN MARRIAGE

ENHANCING INTIMACY IN MARRIAGE

A Clinician's Guide

Dennis A. Bagarozzi, PhD

Human Resources Consultants

Atlanta, GA and Athens, GA

USA	Publishing Office:	BRUNNER-ROUTLEDGE
		A member of the Taylor & Francis Group
		29 West 35th Street
		New York, NY 10001
		Tel: (212) 216-7800
		Fax: (212) 564-7854
	Distribution Center:	BRUNNER-ROUTLEDGE
		A member of the Taylor & Francis Group
		7625 Empire Drive
		Florence, KY 41042
		Tel: 1-800-634-7064
		Fax: 1-800-248-4724
UK		BRUNNER-ROUTLEDGE
		A member of the Taylor & Francis Group
		27 Church Road
		Hove
		E. Sussex, BN3 2FA
		Tel: +44 (0) 1273 207411
		Fax: +44 (0) 1273 205612

ENHANCING INTIMACY IN MARRIAGE: A Clinician's Guide

1 2 3 4 5 6 7 8 9 0

Printed by Sheridan Books, Ann Arbor, MI, 2001.
Cover design by Nancy Abbott.

A CIP catalog record for this book is available from the British Library.
ⓧ The paper in this publication meets the requirements of the ANSI Standard Z39.48-1984 (Permanence of Paper).

Library of Congress Cataloging-in-Publication Data
Bagarozzi, Dennis A.
    Enhancing intimacy in marriage : a clinician's guide / Dennis A. Bagarozzi.
      p. cm.
    Includes bibliographical references.
    ISBN 1-58391-060-3 (case : alk. paper)
    1. Sex instruction. 2. Sex in marriage. 3. Intimacy (Psychology) I. Title.

HQ31 .B197 2001
306.81—dc21

2001027745

ISBN 1-58391-060-3 (case)

CONTENTS

PREFACE

This book was written for clinicians who would like to gain additional knowledge and expertise in the use of some new assessment tools, diagnostic procedures, and intervention techniques for working with couples who present for therapy with intimacy problems as a major source of their marital difficulties. Although some couples may not specifically target intimacy, per se, as a critical issue in their marriage, these same couples will often identify one or more of intimacy's component needs as being problematic for them when they are asked to complete standardized measures of marital quality, satisfaction, or adjustment. When intimacy problems are identified through routine pre-treatment assessments, therapists may wish to consider using some of the diagnostic tools and clinical procedures described in this text to help couples tackle this very important and sensitive problem area.

At the beginning of each chapter, a brief outline is presented. Here the salient topics of discussion are listed for the reader's easy reference. It is important to keep in mind, however, that the clinical techniques described in each chapter are generic in nature, namely, they are not component-need specific. It would be erroneous for the reader to conclude, from reading chapter examples, that a particular intervention strategy must always be used to help couples deal with a specific component-need problem or problem area. How, when, why, and if a therapist decides to use a given technique with a specific couple will depend upon a variety of factors and circumstances. Such decisions are ultimately a matter of clinical judgment, and the author believes that such decisions are best left to the therapist's discretion. Although a student in training or a beginning therapist might take some comfort in the apparent security of a prescriptive approach to treating intimacy problems, the interventions discussed in this book are not meant to be applied rigidly or in accordance with some preconceived formula. As is the case with most clinical techniques, flexibility and common sense in their application are necessary. Therapists who read this volume are encouraged to experiment and creatively use these techniques in ways that are compatible with their own unique styles of conducting therapy.

THEORETICAL
CONSIDERATIONS

CHAPTER 1

Intimacy: Components of a Basic Human Need

☐ Overview

- Intimacy: Examples and definition
- Nine components of intimacy as conceptualized by the author
- Discussion of each component need
- Discussion of romantic love
- Basic ingredients of mature love

☐ Intimacy: Examples and Definitions

John and Susan

John and his wife, Susan, are both retired. They are sitting on a sofa watching videotapes of their grandchildren. Susan rests her head on John's shoulder. John strokes her hair and says pensively: "I am so glad I met you that summer. You have been a wonderful wife for forty years. You've been a loving mother to our children and a caring grandmother. No man could ever ask for more."

Susan is silent for a moment, then she squeezes John's hand and kisses his cheek. "Thank you John," she whispers, "I love you more than words can say."

Jan and Victor

Jan and Victor have been trying for some time to have a child, but have not been successful. In a discouraged voice, Jan says to her husband: "I wonder if my inability to conceive is God's punishment for sins I have committed in my past?"

Victor kisses Jan's forehead, then he gently wipes away her tears and says softly: "God's compassion and forgiveness are infinite. God loves you, and so do I."

Tammy Jane and Cody

Tammy Jane is a professional cowgirl and barrel racer. Cody rides bulls for a living. These two young people refer to their lovemaking as their "midnight rodeo." In the heat of passion, as Tammy Jane approaches orgasm she cries out: "Ride me, cowboy. I'm comin' out of the chute, ride me hard!" Cody pulls Tammy Jane closer to him, looks into her eyes, and laughs.

Matthew and Katie

Matthew lays asphalt all day. He works long, hard hours. Katie often gives Matthew a massage before they retire for the evening. As she rubs his neck and upper back, Katie can feel him begin to relax as the day's tension flows out of his body. In a few minutes, Matthew is fast asleep. Katie kisses the back of his neck, pulls the covers over the two of them and curls up next to her husband and closes her eyes.

Kathy and Robert

Kathy is an attorney in private practice. Robert is a county commissioner. They are childless by choice; a decision they made before they were married. Robert favors a new county legislative proposal that would increase taxes for the purpose of funding secondary education. Kathy, on the other hand, is against the proposal. She tells Robert that she does not believe that childless couples or couples who do not have children enrolled in the public school system should be "burdened with additional taxes." Robert responds by saying "it is everyone's responsibility to provide for the education of the next generation." Kathy smiles at Robert and says: "I guess this is one of those areas where we disagree." Robert looks at Kathy for a second and then says, "One of the things I really admire about you, Kathy, is your consistency and intellectual honesty."

George and Sara

George is late for dinner again, and Sara is angry. As he walks in the front door, Sara says in a calm, measured tone, "George, I am very upset. This is the third time this week that you have come home late. You said you would call me if you were delayed. You show me no consideration. We both work, and I rush home to cook each evening. You make little effort to help me with the work around here. I am frustrated and hurt, and very disappointed in you."

George is silent for a few seconds, then he turns to look at Sara and says in an angry voice, "You never liked my friends. You don't like when I stop to have a few drinks with them after a hard day's work. You say you're upset, well, I'm upset too. Just because we are married now doesn't give you the right to pick my friends and to tell me when to be home, where to go, or what to do."

Sara looks at George intently and says, "George, we have a serious problem in our relationship. We seem to want different things from our marriage." George responds less angrily this time, but he is clearly upset: "Yes, I agree we have some serious problems and some serious differences. I have been wondering if it was a mistake to have married."

James and Connie

James kisses Connie's cheek while she is sleeping. In response to his kiss, Connie opens her eyes and says "good morning." James says "I'm sorry, I did not mean to wake you." Connie replies: "That's O.K. I was not asleep. I was just lying here listening to the geese flying over our house. They really are a vocal group and early risers!"

James leaves their bedroom and begins to prepare their morning coffee. Out of the corner of his eye, he sees something moving quietly through the wood behind their home. It is a doe and her fawn. They have come to drink from the creek which runs through the woods. Softly, James calls Connie to the kitchen window and shows her the two deer. James and Connie watch silently as these two graceful creatures turn to look in their direction. Then, as quietly as they appeared, the doe and her fawn move on and fade into the woods.

James whispers, "They are beautiful," and Connie smiles.

The above vignettes are examples of simple, everyday interpersonal exchanges that occur in the lives of many couples. At first glance, they appear to be unremarkable. However, upon closer examination, one discovers that something very significant has taken place. All of the couples in these examples are engaged in intimate exchanges. Each dialogue demonstrates different types of intimate transactions.

The *Random House Dictionary of the English Language* defines intimacy as a "close, familiar and usually affectionate or loving personal relationship with another person" that entails a "detailed knowledge or deep understanding" of the other person as well as an active expression of one's thoughts and feelings which then serve as a "token of familiarity."

☐ **Nine Components of Intimacy**

One can see from this very concise and pointed definition that true intimacy is an interactive process that contains a number of interrelated components. Central to the process is knowledge, understanding, and acceptance of the other, as well as empathy for the other person's feelings and an appreciation for his or her unique view of the world. The author has worked with couples for more than thirty years, and during this time has identified nine separate, yet interrelated, components or dimensions of intimacy.

These are:

1. Emotional Intimacy
2. Psychological Intimacy
3. Intellectual Intimacy
4. Sexual Intimacy
5. Physical (Nonsexual) Intimacy
6. Spiritual Intimacy
7. Aesthetic Intimacy
8. Social and Recreational Intimacy
9. Temporal Intimacy

In the first example, John and Susan share a moment of physical and emotional intimacy. The interactions between Jan and Victor combine physical, spiritual, and psychological intimacies. Tammy Jane and Cody, on the other hand, show how sexual intimacy often merges with recreational intimacy. Although Matthew and Katie do not verbalize their loving and caring feelings in this example of physical intimacy, it is clear that they share deep and tender feelings for each other. Kathy and Robert's intellectual exchanges also are intimate even though they express very different views. Here we see how mutual respect, empathy, and role reversal are integral parts of a truly intimate relationship. George and Sara are also involved in an emotionally intimate interaction. Even though the feelings expressed are not positive ones, the exchange is still intimate. In the final example, James and Connie share a few brief moments of aesthetic intimacy.

Intimacy is conceptualized as being a basic human need. It is not merely something that one "wants," "desires," or "would like to have." It is a true human need that has its origins in and grows out of a more fundamental survival need for attachment. Severe disruptions in the mother-infant attachment bond or failure of attachment in infancy, for whatever reason, will have dire consequences for the development of true intimacy later in life. (Ainsworth, Blehar, Waters, & Wall, 1978; Bowlby, 1969,

1973, 1979, 1980, 1988; Brazelton & Cramer, 1990; Doane & Diamond, 1994; Horner, 1984; Maccoby & Masters, 1970). The need for intimacy can be conceptualized as a developmentally more mature, differentiated, and advanced manifestation of the universal biological need for physical closeness, connection, and contact with another human being. However, the overall strength of this need for human bonding differs for each individual, and the nine components of this more general need also vary and differ in strength from person to person. So, for example, two people whose overall needs for intimacy are similar in strength may differ drastically in the strengths of their nine separate component needs. When one considers these differences between individuals, it is easy to understand how a husband and a wife, or two lovers, whose overall needs for intimacy are similar in strength, may still be dissatisfied with the intimacy they share and experience in their relationship. Frequently, couples who enter therapy in order to deal with dissatisfactions that revolve around unmet intimacy needs are surprised to learn that their differences in *overall needs strengths* and *component needs strengths* are simply that—namely, differences. Unfortunately, many couples interpret these differences as being "good" or "bad," "healthy" or "neurotic," "desirable" or "undesirable," etc. One of the primary tasks of a therapist who works with couples having difficulties in this area of their relationship is to help them understand and accept, if possible, their needs strengths differences.

For purposes of clarity, the nine components of intimacy are presented below as ideal types:

Emotional Intimacy

Emotional Intimacy is the need for communicating and sharing with one's partner all of one's feelings, both positive (e.g., happiness, joy, elation, gladness, excitement) and negative (e.g., sadness, unhappiness, frustration, fear, anger, guilt, shame, loneliness, boredom, fatigue, depression).

For emotional intimacy to be achieved, there should be few prohibitions or limitations placed upon the feelings that are permitted expression in a relationship. If, for example, only positive emotions are allowed expression, then an artificially positive atmosphere will exist in the relationship. If, on the other hand, only negative emotions are allowed expression then the overall emotional atmosphere of the relationship will be one of doom and gloom. In some instances, however, the couple's unverbalized rule system may restrict emotional expression. In such arrangements, the full depth or height, as well as the range of emotional expression, may be constricted. For example, partners may express happiness or joy but not elation or excitement, or a partner may be able to show frustration and annoyance but not anger. Similarly, a person may feel free to express sadness, but depression and despondency are off limits.

Psychological Intimacy

Psychological Intimacy is the need to communicate, share, and connect with another human being by disclosing deeply significant and personally meaningful material about one's true and inner self. Psychological intimacy encompasses the need to share and express one's hopes, dreams, fantasies, aspirations, and plans for the future as well as sharing one's fears, concerns, doubts, insecurities, problems, and inner conflicts with one's partner. The type of sharing that takes place during a psychologically intimate moment is one that makes the sharer vulnerable. Pretense and defensiveness are incompatible with psychological sharing and disclosure. The sharer risks being totally exposed and transparent during psychologically intimate moments. In order for true psychological intimacy to exist, there must be a secure base of trust in the relationship. Each partner must feel safe in sharing his or her innermost self without the fear of being judged, evaluated, ridiculed, shamed, scorned, demeaned, or punished for these revelations. Opening oneself up to another, in this intimate way, renders one psychologically naked.

Intellectual Intimacy

Intellectual Intimacy is the need to communicate and share important ideas, thoughts, and beliefs with one's partner. Intellectual intimacy should not be confused with the unconscious defense mechanism of intellectualization which is used to avoid feeling certain emotions; to demonstrate one's intellectual superiority; to gain praise, recognition, or adulation. Intellectualization is designed to create a distance (usually a status difference) between individuals, and works in direct opposition to increasing true intimacy. In order for intellectual intimacy to take place, respect for the other's viewpoint must be present, especially respect for the other's opposing or differing views. A critical component of intellectual intimacy is one's *role-taking* ability. Role taking is the ability to view the world through the eyes of one's partner, to perceive what one's partner perceives from the other person's unique vantage point, and to reverse perspectives so that one can see oneself as one is seen by one's partner. This ability to de-center and reverse perspectives is critical for the development of true intellectual intimacy. The emotional counterpart of role taking is *empathy*.

Empathy is the ability to put oneself in another's place, to feel what the other person must be feeling, but not to identify with the other or feel sorry (have sympathy) for the other. Empathy for the feelings of one's partner (or for any other person) can be considered a *meta-emotion*, namely, a caring emotional response about another person's feelings. Any time empathy is felt and expressed in a relationship, the exchange is enriched by adding the dimension of emotional intimacy.

Empathy and role taking are essential to the development of true intimacy; their importance in the development of true intimacy is second only to mutual trust and respect.

Sexual Intimacy

Sexual Intimacy is the need for communicating, sharing, and expressing with one's partner those thoughts, feelings, desires, and fantasies that are of a sensual and sexual nature. Intimacy of this type is engaged in specifically for the purpose of arousing sexual desire. Sexually arousing activities might include such experiences as watching erotic films, videotapes, or live performances together. Listening to or playing music that has sexually suggestive or sexually explicit lyrics, reading prose or poetry with or to one's partner that is intended to produce sexual arousal is also an aspect of sexual intimacy. Sexual intimacy includes the need and desire to engage in acts of physical closeness and bodily contact such as touching and fondling that are specifically designed to be sexually stimulating, exciting, pleasing, and satisfying for both the person performing these acts and the recipient of these behaviors. Kissing, hugging, holding, petting, dancing, horseplay, bathing, and so forth that is intended to cause sexual arousal are additional aspects of sexual intimacy. Genital touching or stimulation by oneself or by one's partner may or may not be part of a sexually intimate experience. Similarly, sexual intimacy may or may not lead to intercourse or orgasm for one or both partners.

Sexual intimacy is usually thought to be a central component of erotic/romantic love but is considered to be distinct and different from other forms of love such as maternal love, paternal love, fraternal (brotherly) love, sororal (sisterly) love, familial love, philanthropic love (love for the human race), love of one's country, platonic love, love of God, the love that God has for humankind (agape), and self-love (i.e., a positive valuing of one's self, self-respect, and self-esteem that is not defensive or false, and a concern for one's self that is neither narcissistic nor lacking in empathy for others).

Erotic/romantic love is often a central component of conjugal love (i.e., the love shared between a husband and wife) in most Western cultures.

However, societies do exist where erotic/romantic love is not considered to be a prerequisite for marriage and may not even be considered an essential part of the conjugal relationship.

Erotic/romantic love is predominantly a subjective *emotional* experience that entails a longing to be united with the object of one's affection. Feelings of loss, loneliness, and sadness are usually accompanied by a sense of incompleteness and emptiness in erotic/romantic love. A major characteristic of erotic/romantic love is the overwhelming desire to be sexually intimate with one's lover. Sometimes there is a desire for complete and utter union with one's partner so much so that one's personal ego boundaries become blurred or dissolved and the lovers' identities temporarily merge and become one.

In erotic/romantic love, one's partner is idealized and idolized. To be loved by one's partner in a similar fashion is thought and felt to be necessary to sustain one's happiness and to maintain one's personal existence. A truly romantic idea in heterosexual love is the belief that total union in all areas of intimacy with a person of the opposite sex completes the self. Through such a union, a woman is able to integrate her unrealized and underdeveloped masculine self—her Animus. Similarly, a man deeply involved in erotic/romantic love finds his unrealized and underdeveloped feminine self (his Anima) through his union with his lover.

There are several myths that nurture and fuel erotic/romantic love. These are:

1. We fall in love. Love is an *emotion* over which we have no control. It is a deeply mystical experience—a desire so strong that one cannot be held responsible or accountable for one's actions while under its influence. One is drunk with love, madly in love, hopelessly in love, under the spell of love, etc.
2. Since erotic/romantic love is mystical, mysterious, and beyond our control, we cannot choose with whom we fall in love, nor can we predict where or when we might fall. There is a fatal and fatalistic aura surrounding erotic/romantic love.
3. There is only one special person put on this earth specifically intended to be one's true love, one's soul mate, and one's partner for life. Although one may fall in love many times during one's life, there is really only one true love. The belief that only true love will bring a person happiness may cause some people to spend their entire lives moving from one relationship to another searching for their true love with the hope of "living happily ever after."
4. All you need is love. Love will conquer all. No matter what adversities or obstacles lovers encounter in life, love will see them through. If the couple cannot weather these storms, then it must not have been true love.

Conjugal love, as mentioned earlier, often includes aspects of erotic/romantic love. This usually occurs in the early stages of relationship formation and development, but conjugal love cannot be sustained solely by erotic/romantic love and passion. Conjugal love is much more encompassing and complex. Conjugal love is a condition that can exist between two individuals who are not formally or legally married; therefore, the term *mature love* is used in its place. The cornerstone of a mature love relationship is a free and willing commitment to the other person as well as a commitment to the growth and development of the relationship as a whole.

Mature love has components that one also finds in maternal and paternal forms of love, for example, a love where the well-being and happiness of the other is essential to one's own well-being and happiness.

The basic ingredients of mature love are described below:

1. *In-depth knowledge of the other*. In order to love another, one must know who that person truly is. Essentially, mature love comes from knowing the person in all the nine domains of intimacy that are the subjects of this book. In mature love, the other is known and loved for who he or she is and not for what he or she possesses (physical qualities, material possessions, and so on). In mature love, the real person, with all his or her faults and imperfections, is cared for. There is no need for improvement in mature love. The person is not loved because of what he or she might become in the future. The person is loved for how he or she is in the present and not for his or her potential to be something different.

2. *Respect for the other*. Closely linked to knowledge of the other is respect. Respect here means respect for the other person as a different and unique human being. The other is not seen as a projection or an extension of the self. The other is not a carbon copy of the self. The other is loved because he or she is different, not in spite of his or her differences. Any attempt to change the other is an act of disrespect. One can respect another only if there is respect for oneself.

3. *Acceptance of the other*. Acceptance is similar to respect in that there is no attempt to change the other person. However, acceptance of the other does not mean an unqualified acceptance of those behaviors that are incompatible with a loving relationship. Like intimacy, a loving relationship is mutual and reciprocal, not one-sided. In a mature, loving relationship, a person treats his or her partner in a way that he or she would like to be treated. Acceptance of another, like respect, can only occur if one accepts himself or herself. In this sense, acceptance is not earned. It is given unconditionally. However, acceptance of the other can be lost if trust is broken and honesty is not forthcoming.

4. *Trust and honesty*. Trust and honesty go hand in hand. Although these

two constructs are conceptually distinct, they are closely tied together. Trust is based upon the premise that the other person will honor his or her commitments reliably and consistently over time. Honesty means that what a person says is factually true and accurate, and that there is no conscious effort to deceive the other. Therefore, a statement made by one partner to another can be taken at face value. This issue is addressed in Chapter 2 in the discussion of functional and dysfunctional communication. Trust and honesty are linked by behavior. There should be congruence between what one says and what one does, with no room for doubt. Mature love can develop only between two individuals who have successfully separated and individuated from their primary caretakers and families of origin, have solidified a positive identity, and have developed a fully integrated self. In mature love, both partners understand the fine distinctions between responsibility *to* one's partner and responsibility *for* one's partner. Similarly, in a mature love relationship, both individuals know the difference between caring *for* one's partner and taking care *of* one's mate. Furthermore, they are able to recognize when it is appropriate to take care of one's partner (e.g., in times of illness, grief, crisis) and when it is not. Finally, a loving and caring relationship requires some degree of appropriate *interdependence*. This interdependence is in no way pathological or neurotic and is more like dependability—that is, trust. A person can count on his or her partner to fulfill his or her part of the relationship contract.

Conflicts, problems, and differences of opinion are normal and expected parts of any long-term and committed relationship. In and of themselves, such difficulties do not interfere with intimacy and they do not pose a problem in a relationship where there is mature love, understanding, and empathy. Conflicts are accepted as an unpleasant part of living one's life with another human being. It is at such times in a relationship when commitment to the other person plays a major role. Both individuals in a mature love relationship are committed as a couple to resolving their differences, solving their problems, and negotiating conflicts in a way that does not require one partner to lose at the other's expense. Essentially, the partners approach their interpersonal difficulties as a collaborative team whose ultimate goal is a mutually satisfying resolution to their problems, conflicts, and differences.

Physical (Nonsexual) Intimacy

Physical Intimacy is the need for physical closeness with one's partner. Physical closeness of this type should not be confused with physical intimacy that is intended to produce or accompany sexual arousal. Physical intimacy may be expressed by a simple touch, or it may include close bodily contact such as a hug. Physical intimacy includes such experiences as holding hands, cuddling together, dancing with one's partner and non-sexual touching. Kissing that is not a prelude to sexual relations, sleeping with one's partner, walking arm-in-arm, giving one's partner a back rub or massage, and so on, are all part of physical non-sexual intimacy.

Spiritual Intimacy

Spiritual Intimacy is the need to share one's thoughts, feelings, beliefs, and experiences with one's partner that have to do with religion, the supernatural and spiritual realms of existence, moral values and beliefs, the meaning of existence, life after death, one's relationship to God or a higher power, one's relationship to nature, and one's place in the cosmos. Spirituality may or may not be tied to a recognized or organized religion or to any ritualized practice or group of practices. Spirituality is a highly individual and personal matter. It may include, however, the joint practice and participation in religious or spiritual activities, rituals, or celebrations, together with one's partner. Spiritual intimacy between two people does not require that they be of the same faith or subscribe to similar belief systems for genuinely intimate experiences to take place. What is necessary, however, is a sincere openness to the other's spiritual beliefs, feelings, and experiences, and respect for the other's spiritual world. As is true for all dimensions of intimacy, nonjudgmental acceptance of the other's viewpoints and beliefs is essential. For some individuals, the spiritual dimension of themselves is a central component of their identity. When the spiritual part of one's makeup constitutes a core aspect of the self, disclosures about this part of one's being moves intimacy into the realm of a holy or sacred experience. For the person whose life path is a spiritual one, sharing in this dimension may represent the most profound form of intimacy.

Aesthetic Intimacy

Aesthetic Intimacy is the need and desire to share with one's partner feelings, thoughts, perceptions, beliefs, and experiences that one considers to be personally moving, breathtaking, or awe inspiring because of their beauty. The wonders of nature, both simple (a snowflake) and complex (the cosmos) can form the basis for such experiential intimacy. Music, poetry, literature, painting, sculpture, architecture, and all forms of artistic expression can serve as media for aesthetic sharing. In aesthetic intimacy, the beauty of the experience is shared for its own sake. The aesthetic experience is a pure experience. It is not used as a prelude to other types of intimate experiences nor is it enjoyed as an accompaniment for other forms of intimate expression.

Social and Recreational Intimacy

Social and Recreational Intimacy is the need to engage in playful and enjoyable activities and experiences with one's partner. Social and recreational intimacy with one's partner includes activities and experiences such as: exchanging jokes and humorous stories; sharing one's daily experiences and discussing current events; sharing meals, snacks and refreshments; exercising together; playing sports and games together; sharing hobbies; dancing together for pleasure; gardening; boating; vacationing together, and so on. Social and recreational intimacy may include activities and interactions with mutual friends and other family members.

Temporal Intimacy

Temporal Intimacy involves how much time each partner would like to spend with his or her mate, on a daily basis, in intimate activities. Not surprisingly, it is not uncommon to find that the amount of time one needs to spend each day with his or her partner in order to feel intimately connected differs from individual to individual, and the types of activities one would like to engage in with one's partner in order to feel intimately related to him or her also differ from person to person. For some individuals, 15 or 20 minutes each day may be sufficient. For others, however, two or three hours each day may seem too little.

By now the reader has begun to realize that the more two individuals differ in their component needs strengths, the less likely they will be to feel satisfied with the intimacy they experience in their relationship.

Intimacy: An Interactive and Dynamic Process

☐ Overview

- Intimate relationships history outline
- Critical periods for the development of intimacy
- Major developmental tasks associated with intimacy
- Romantic relationships history outline
- The dynamics of intimacy
- Component and overall intimacy needs strengths
- Case example of needs strengths differences: Mike and Jane
- Receptivity and Reciprocity satisfactions
- Communication and intimacy: Functional and dysfunctional patterns and styles

In Chapter 1 we saw that intimacy is made up of nine different, yet closely related, component needs that vary in strength from individual to individual. In work with couples who desire to achieve deeper levels of intimacy, it is helpful to conduct a detailed history of each partner's intimate relationships. Since intimacy needs evolve out of the more primary need for attachment, it is appropriate to find out, as much as possible, about each partner's earliest relationship with his or her primary caretaker. Ainsworth et al. (1978) identified several types of primary patterns of infant-mother attachment, namely, secure, insecure-ambivalent-resistant, insecure-avoidant, and insecure-disorganized. These early attachment patterns are introjected and incorporated into the individual's psychic struc-

15

ture where they serve as "internal working models of attachment" (Bowlby, 1969, 1973, 1979, 1980, 1988). These internal working models can be thought of as affectively laden cognitive structures that remain fairly stable throughout the person's life (Slade & Arber, 1992). Successful separation-individuation is fostered by the caretaker's encouragement of the child's budding independence. If the child has a secure base from which to venture out and to which he or she can return whenever necessary, a healthy balance of separateness and connectedness is established between the child and the primary attachment figures (Bowlby, 1988; Mahler, Pine, & Bergman, 1975) which then serves as a paradigm for future intimate relationships. Any history of intimate relationships, therefore, should begin with an exploration of each partner's relationship with his or her primary caretaker. Since this primary attachment figure usually is the child's mother, the mother-child relationship should be the first relationship explored.

Information about early infant-mother attachment can be gathered from a variety of sources. The primary source for such information would be the mother herself. In cases where this is not possible, for whatever reason, reports about the mother-infant relationship can be obtained from the father, older siblings, and other relatives who were on hand to observe this early relationship.

The individual's earliest memories about his or her relationship with his or her mother are important. Even if these are not factually accurate, they are valuable because they represent the individual's internal working model of attachment.

Another source of information would be videotapes of early mother-infant interactions (e.g., delivery, birth, nursing). Written material serves as another source of data, for example, parents' recollections recorded in baby books where developmental milestones were described. Especially helpful would be any information about the child's temperament and his or her need for physical closeness with the mother. Letters written about the child by his or her parents and stories about the child that have become part of family lore and mythology (Bagarozzi & Anderson, 1989) can also shed some light on early attachments and relationship patterns.

Clearly, any disruptions or trauma that might have affected the mother-child bond (e.g., death, illness, long hospitalization, psychiatric illnesses, separation during critical periods, abandonment, physical or sexual abuse, or neglect) should be explored in depth in order to assess their possible impact upon the person's ability to form secure attachments.

The nature and quality of each partner's relationship with other significant family members, friends, and caretakers should be the next group of associations explored. Special attention should be given to each partner's parents' relationship, because how an individual learns about intimate male-female relationships is greatly influenced by his or her observations, perceptions, and interpretations of his or her parents' relationship. Similarly, any significant male-female relationships that might have served as models for intimacy should be explored.

For most people, the capacity for developing intimate relationships begins at about the age of 6 or 7. Prior to this time, most children have not matured sufficiently in those critical areas of personality and cognitive development that are considered to be prerequisites for beginning this lifelong process. Harry Stack Sullivan (1953), the pioneering psychiatrist and personality theorist, believed that middle and later childhood (ages 6–12) are critical times for setting the foundation for the development of true intimacy later in life. Sullivan identified four developmental process tasks that children must master if they are to become fully functioning persons capable of having fulfilling and rewarding multifaceted, intimate relationships as adults. These process tasks are:

1. The ability to engage in competitive activities with peers.
2. The ability to compromise with one's peers.
3. The ability to collaborate with one's peers.
4. The ability to cooperate with one's peers.

Significant relationships with same-sex peers during this important stage of interpersonal and personal development, therefore, constitute the next area of investigation. It is during this stage of the life cycle that the capacity for empathy and role taking begins to develop.

Empathy (feeling what it must be like to be in another person's shoes) and role taking (seeing the world from another person's unique perspective) are two abilities without which true intimacy cannot be achieved. Material gathered during this history-taking process concerning the nature and quality of same-sex peer relationships will provide valuable information about each partner's success in mastering these essential tasks and acquiring the cognitive and socioemotional skills that are needed to have a multifaceted mature intimate relationship later in adult life.

In Western cultures, for the most part, adolescence is the time when many young people begin to associate with and date members of the opposite sex. Learning how to have a multifaceted intimate (and not simply sexual) relationship with a member of the opposite sex, while still maintaining close and intimate relationships with same-sex peers, at the same time that one is struggling to find his or her own separate identity is a difficult and daunting task. Nevertheless, learning how to become truly intimate with a member of the opposite sex is a necessary developmental task of adolescence (Erikson, 1968). Accomplishing this task is essential if one is to have a truly intimate relationship with one's partner later in life. When exploring the heterosexual relationships that occurred during an individual's adolescence, it is important to ask about all significant heterosexual friendships in addition to those relationships that were predominantly romantic and/or sexual in nature. In the author's clinical experience, it has been found that individuals who have had close and intimate nonsexual relationships with members of the opposite sex during adolescence have little difficulty developing multifaceted intimate heterosexual relationships in adult life. On the other hand, individuals who have not had such experiences with members of the opposite sex during this critical period are frequently those who have intimacy problems later in life. In many cases, these individuals are truly baffled when their partners complain about the "lack of intimacy" in their marriage or relationship. For these individuals, if they are engaging in sexual intercourse with their partners, they consider their relationships to be intimate. Although men are more prone to think and feel this way, the author has, in his practice, encountered a number of women who share this viewpoint.

The final area to be explored when taking a history of intimate relationships is that of long-term romantic relationships. Tracing the development of these relationships over the course of time, beginning with the earliest one and ending with the current relationship, completes the process. A number of important processes and critical incidents should be investigated. Some of the major factors to consider are:

1. How did each relationship begin?
2. Who initiated the dating process?
3. What were the factors, personality traits, physical appearance, and so on, that attracted the person to his or her partner?
4. How long did each relationship last?
5. What was the predominant affective tone and overall quality of each relationship?
6. Were there any significant problems in the relationship and did any of these problems cause the couple to separate or breakup for a period of time? How frequently did this occur? How long did each breakup last? Who initiated the reconciliation?
7. How were conflicts and disagreements resolved in each relationship?
8. Were there any significant differences in the needs for intimacy and interpersonal closeness in any of these relationships? If there were, which areas of needs differences became a problem and caused conflicts in the relationship? How were these needs differences dealt with, and how were these conflicts resolved?

9. In addition to differences in intimacy needs, did any of the following factors or issues become a source of conflict in these past relationships?
   (a) Trust
   (b) Commitment
   (c) Honesty
   (d) Fidelity
   (e) Jealousy
   (f) Betrayal of a nonsexual nature
   (g) Respect
   (h) Interpersonal violence
   (i) Substance abuse
   (j) Finances
   (k) Religious beliefs
   (l) Children (in the case of previous marriages)

☐ The Dynamics of Intimacy: Receptivity and Reciprocity

Intimacy is a dynamic and interactive process that is based upon mutual trust and respect. Therefore, each partner must feel totally secure in sharing his or her deepest thoughts and feelings with his or her mate, without any fear of being judged, evaluated, or ridiculed. In addition to knowing that one's partner is fully *receptive* to whatever is shared and disclosed, a person must also feel that his or her partner is *reciprocating* (i.e., giving back in return) similar depth levels of self-disclosure, self-revelation, etc., in order for intimacy to continue to develop. It is this *mutuality of receptivity and reciprocity* that allows the relationship to move into deeper levels of trust and love.

In order to determine whether one's intimacy needs are being met sufficiently by one's partner, four interrelated factors must be considered and evaluated. These are:

1. Overall intimacy needs strengths of both partners.
2. The strength of each component need for both partners.
3. Each partner's satisfaction with his or her mate's openness, receptivity, responsiveness, willingness, and ability to meet and satisfy each specific component need.
4. Each partner's satisfaction with his or her mate's willingness and ability to reciprocate similar depth levels of sharing, openness, self-disclosure, self-revelation, and personal exchange.

Each of these factors is discussed below.

☐ Overall Intimacy Needs Strengths of the Partner

By the time a person reaches adulthood, the strength of his or her intimacy needs, in all component areas, have become fairly well established. Although the author has not yet conducted longitudinal research, and therefore does not have empirical evidence to support his observations, it appears that the overall strength of a person's needs for intimacy does not change substantially throughout the course of adult life. This trait-like aspect of intimacy is important to keep in mind, because substantial intimacy needs differences between partners are not likely to change. Such intimacy needs discrepancies, once identified through testing, must be squarely faced by any couple contemplating marriage or a permanent relationship.

☐ Component Needs Strengths Differences: Further Considerations

As was mentioned earlier in Chapter 1, partners with similar overall intimacy needs strengths may still experience the amount, type, depth, and frequency of intimately shared experiences they have together to be unfulfilling and unsatisfying. This often happens whenever partners have wide needs strengths discrepancies for the same component needs. Such component needs strengths discrepancies are especially troubling and problematic when the specific needs in question are experienced by the person as being central to that individual's self, identity, character, or personality makeup. For example, Mike and Jane were referred to the author's Premarital Education and Training Sequence (PETS) program by their pastor. As a routine part of this premarital counseling program, Mike and Jane completed the Intimacy Needs Survey. The Intimacy Needs Survey was developed in 1990 as a clinical aid designed to help couples assess the degree to which they were satisfied with the intimacy they shared in their relationships (a full discussion of the Intimacy Needs Survey is provided in Chapter 3).

The Total Intimacy Needs Strength scores and the Component Needs Strengths scores for Mike and Jane are shown in Table 2.1, opposite.

At first glance, the difference between Mike's low average Total Intimacy Needs Strength score and Jane's high average Total Intimacy Needs Strength score do not appear to be very great. Statistically their numerical scores were not significantly different. However, the differences in their Component Needs Strength scores were very significant and meaningful personally for Jane. Her need for frequent and intense emotional

TABLE 2.1.

Component Needs Strengths	Mike	Jane
1. Emotional Intimacy	Low	High
2. Psychological Intimacy	Average	Average
3. Intellectual Intimacy	High	Average
4. Spiritual Intimacy	Average	Average
5. Sexual Intimacy	Low	High
6. Aesthetic Intimacy	Average	Low
7. Social/Recreational Intimacy	High	Average
8. Physical (Nonsexual) Intimacy	Low	High
Total Intimacy Needs Strength	Low Average	High Average

exchanges with Mike, her strong sex drive, and her high need for close physical contact were central components of Jane's personality makeup; they were part of her identity as a mature woman. Although Jane loved Mike deeply, and she knew he returned her love, she still felt "unconnected" to him. She felt cut off from him in three very important areas of her life.

Mike loved Jane dearly. He was devoted to her and would have done anything within his power to make her happy. Unfortunately, he could not satisfy Jane's intimacy needs in these three critical areas, no matter how hard he tried. Although Mike made a sincere effort to feel more deeply and to express his feelings to Jane, his attempts felt artificial to both of them. Mike also tried to be more physically demonstrative with Jane even though this physical closeness sometimes made him feel smothered and uncomfortable. Sadly, as one would expect, Mike's sex drive remained essentially the same even though he made a concerted effort to engage in intercourse with Jane more frequently.

In order to help couples who have major discrepancies in the strengths of their component needs for intimacy appreciate the scope and depth of their differences, the author asks them to complete a "pie chart" exercise. The pie chart exercise is simple. Each partner is given an 8½ × 11 inch sheet of paper upon which is drawn a complete circle. The partners are asked to pretend that the circle represents the totality of their intimacy needs. Each partner is then instructed to divide the "pie" into eight pieces and to make each piece correspond in size to each component intimacy need.

Mike and Jane's pie charts are reproduced on the following page in Figures 2.1 and 2.2:

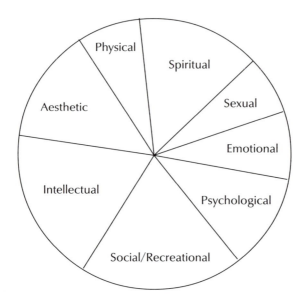

FIGURE 2.1. Mike

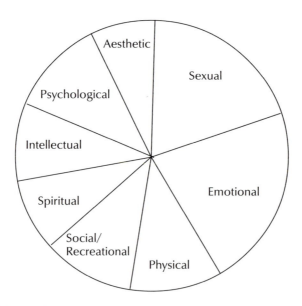

FIGURE 2.2. Jane

Mike's and Jane's pie chart drawings do not correspond perfectly to the scores each of them received on the Intimacy Needs Survey for each of the eight component needs areas of intimacy. Such differences are not uncommon, because they reflect two very different phenomena. Pie chart representations are psychological, subjective, personal, and intuitive expressions of one's inner needs. Essentially, they are products of the brain's right hemisphere. Intimacy Needs Survey scores, on the other hand, are arrived at statistically. Intimacy Needs Survey scores reflect the logic of the left hemisphere. Both sources of information are valid and informative sources of data that complement each other. Taken together, they represent a more complete picture that can help partners appreciate, in graphic detail, the intimacy needs strengths discrepancies that exist between them. Mike and Jane's pie charts were very troubling for them because, for the first time, they were confronted with what they both had already suspected at some unconscious level of awareness: Mike and Jane had significant needs strengths differences in three key areas for Jane (sexual, emotional, and physical intimacy). This graphic and concrete depiction of their differences was disturbing to both of them and caused them to reconsider their decision to marry.

☐ Component Needs Discrepancies and Relationship Satisfaction

From the previous discussion, one might be led to conclude that if two partners have different needs strengths for the same component needs, both partners would automatically feel dissatisfied with the intimacy they share in these areas. As logical as this assumption sounds, clinical data the author has collected over the past nine years do not support it. It is not uncommon to find two partners with component needs strengths discrepancies who consider the intimate exchanges they share in these areas to be rewarding and satisfying. This occurs for a number of reasons:

First, if the need or needs in question are not ones that the person experiences as being central to himself or herself, dissatisfaction will be unlikely provided that his or her partner is able to meet and satisfy those needs that he or she considers to be central to the self and his or her personality makeup.

Second, the discrepancies that do exist may not be large enough to cause concern, because they are not considered to be central to the couple's relationship satisfaction. This is especially true if the need in question can be satisfied by another person or through another relationship, provided that these other people or relationships do not threaten the cohesiveness of the couple's relationship.

Third, most people are reasonable: they do not expect their partners to be able to satisfy totally all their intimacy needs. However, they do expect their partners to be able and willing to satisfy central component needs at some self-determined level of acceptance. Dissatisfaction occurs only when a partner's ability or willingness to satisfy a particular intimacy need or group of needs falls below that person's self-determined critical level of acceptance. As one would expect, these critical acceptance levels for each component need differ from person to person. Satisfaction, when it comes to intimacy, is a highly personal and subjective matter. This subjective evaluation process takes into consideration the two processes of receptivity and reciprocity mentioned earlier. These terms are defined as follows:

Receptivity Satisfaction is the subjective satisfaction one experiences with the degree and quality of acceptance, empathy, and understanding that one's partner shows in response to one's intimate self-disclosures and expression of a felt need.

Reciprocity Satisfaction is the subjective satisfaction one experiences with the depth, extent, and quality of one's partner's self-disclosures and expressions of felt need for the same component need.

Receptivity satisfaction and Reciprocity satisfaction are two qualities also measured by the Intimacy Needs Survey. In work with couples, the author has found that dissatisfaction concerning a partner's ability to meet and gratify a particular component need is often experienced whenever a partner's ability to satisfy his or her mate's *expressed need* (in either receptivity or reciprocity) falls below a 70% self-determined level of acceptance. The reader will note the use of the term *expressed need*. The author makes a distinction between a person's felt need and an expressed need, because a partner should not expect his or her mate to know intuitively or automatically what intimacy need or needs he or she would like to have satisfied at any particular point in time. Such unspoken expectations for mind reading on the part of a partner usually leads to hurt feelings and conflict in a relationship. A direct verbal request for intimate sharing is the best way to make one's intimacy needs known to one's partner.

☐ Communication and Intimacy

The depth of intimacy that two individuals create in their relationship depends, to a large degree, upon their ability to communicate their thoughts, feelings, needs, wants, and desires clearly, accurately, and effectively. Therefore, learning how to communicate functionally is the first step in the process of creating or increasing intimacy in any relationship. Many couples who enter marital counseling or marital therapy in order to deal with intimacy problems in their relationship often cite "poor communication" as the primary reason for their difficulties. Communication problems usually come about whenever the message sent by one partner (the sender) is different from the message heard and received by the other partner (the receiver). Human communication problems, therefore, are of two different types: sender problems or receiver problems. Some of the most common sender and receiver problems are briefly discussed below:

Common Sender Problems

Lying

The easiest type of sender problem to identify is the lie. Essentially, the sender's motive is deception. There is a willful and conscious attempt, on the sender's part, to deceive, mislead, misinform, fool, dupe, or manipulate the receiver. Lying to one's partner clearly strikes at the very heart and soul of intimacy, since when one lies, trust, honesty, and respect are severely compromised. Forgiveness by the offended partner can only be granted when the offending partner (a) acknowledges his or her transgressions, (b) takes full responsibility for his or her behavior, (c) makes amends (and restitution when necessary), (d) asks for forgiveness, (e) agrees to tell the truth in the future, and (f) behaves in accordance with his or her promise to be truthful. Chronic lying is frequently a symptom of severe character pathology. The likelihood of couples developing or regaining true intimacy in their relationship is remote whenever one partner has a history of chronic lying.

Hidden Messages

Sometimes the true meaning of a message is hidden, disguised, or concealed in the actual literal verbal content of the message sent, and the receiver is expected to decode, decipher, understand and then respond to the intended message in a very specific manner. For example, a wife may casually mention that she is "going up to the bedroom to read before retiring for the night." The literal meaning (or the report aspect of the message) is crystal clear. However, the possible hidden meanings (or the command aspect of the message) may be quite different for each partner. The husband may wonder if his wife is telling him that she is tired and is not interested in having sexual relations that evening or whether she is saying that she is now available for lovemaking.

A husband's innocuous comments about the weather, such as, "It is a beautiful day. Not a cloud in the sky" may cause his wife to wonder if he is really asking her if it is O.K. for him to be gone most of the day golfing with his buddies or whether he is actually saying that since the weather has cleared they might be able to go to the seashore for that long-awaited weekend in the sun.

One would have to be a mind reader to know the true meaning of all hidden messages. Sometimes, however, after living with someone for a considerable amount of time, a partner may be able to guess the true meaning of some hidden messages, but the more this type of communication is used in relationships, the more likely confusion, frustration, misunderstanding, and conflict are apt to develop.

People send hidden messages for a variety of reasons—they may be underassertive, they may have been taught that it is impolite to be direct, or they may believe that it is improper to ask for what one desires. Whatever the reason, this type of communication is dysfunctional. Eventually, intimacy will suffer.

Mixed Messages

Mixed messages are messages for which the true meaning is unclear. Since mixed messages are another source of misunderstanding, conflict, and frustration, confusion often develops in relationships where such communications are common. Like messages with hidden meanings, mixed messages have a corrosive effect upon intimacy. Two of the most common types of mixed messages are *sarcastic communications* and *qualified messages*.

Sarcastic communications can be considered indirect expressions of aggression. As such, they represent hostile forms of communicating one's displeasure. Sarcastic messages are usually constructed in a way that is designed to convey a thought, feeling, or meaning that is contrary to or opposite from the message's literal meaning and content. For example, a husband says to his wife "Thank you for your thoughtful gift" in order to express his negative feelings toward her for forgetting his birthday.

The recipient of a sarcastic communication usually experiences some type of negative emotion in response to the hostile remark (e.g., anger, shame, guilt, confusion, embarrassment, annoyance, or frustration). A defensive explanation or an apology may follow the felt emotion. If, however, the receiver of the sarcastic communication responds with a counter-sarcastic retort, a full-blown conflict may ensue. To avoid an all-out confrontation, the sender of a sarcastic message may try to defuse the conflict by proclaiming that the hostile message was "only a joke," thereby taking no responsibility for the aggressive act.

Sarcastic messages usually serve no constructive purpose and only contribute to the erosion of intimacy since they tend to drive a wedge between the partners. Sarcastic remarks are counterproductive because they do not help couples identify the source of conflict in a way that makes it possible for them to negotiate their differences and reach a mutually agreed upon solution to the problem at hand.

The literal meaning of a verbal message can be *qualified* in a number of ways. Verbal tone, volume, quality, and pitch all can be used to qualify the literal meaning of a spoken message. Facial expressions, hand gestures, and body postures also can be used to qualify the meaning of a sender's verbal message. Qualifiers can be either congruent with what was said, or they can be incongruent with what the sender is communicating verbally. A partner's behavior can be consistent (i.e., reliable) or inconsistent (i.e., unreliable) with the spoken message. Congruent nonverbal qualifiers and behaviors that are consistent with the spoken word increase trust in a relationship and foster intimacy. Qualifiers that are incongruent or behaviors that are inconsistent with the verbal message sent by a partner will tend to decrease interpersonal trust. In the following example, a number of nonverbal qualifiers can be identified:

> David tells his wife, Annette, that he is genuinely concerned about the difficulties she is having with her sister. However, when Annette begins to tell him about this painful relationship, she notices that he begins to open the mail, looks at his wristwatch, plays with the family dog, and switches on the television.

Clearly, David's nonverbal behavior is not consistent with his expressed interest. As a result, Annette begins to question David's sincerity and intimacy suffers.

Paradoxical Communications

Paradoxical messages are self-contradictory communications that have an absurd quality about them. Two types of paradoxical communications can be identified in human communication. The first is a *paradoxical self-definition*. An example of a paradoxical self-definition can be seen in the following exchange between Mr. and Mrs. Smith:

> Mrs. Smith: John, before we were married you told me that you had paid off all your credit card debts. Today, I accidentally came across a credit card bill of yours. The balance is six thousand dollars! How do you explain this?
>
> Mr. Smith: I told you before we were married that you should never believe what a Smith tells you.

Obviously, Mrs. Smith is perplexed by her husband's paradoxical self-definition. Her husband is a Smith. If he is lying, he is telling the truth, but if he is telling the truth, he is a liar. Paradoxical self-definitions make it impossible to trust the sender.

The second type of paradoxical communication is a *paradoxical command*. Paradoxical commands are also referred to as paradoxical injunctions. What makes these commands paradoxical is that in order to obey them, one must disobey them. Paradoxical commands are more common than paradoxical self-definitions and are frequently seen in clinical settings. Some common examples are:

1. A domineering husband urges his wife to be more assertive in their marriage.
2. A distressed wife says that she is tired of making all the decisions in the family so she instructs her husband to take more of the initiative in their marriage.
3. A frustrated husband asks his wife to ignore what he says.

Aggressive Messages

Any form of communication (verbal, nonverbal, physical) that is consciously and willfully intended to harm another individual is considered to be an aggressive communication. Clearly, aggressive messages will have a negative impact upon intimacy. Since trust and security are cornerstones of an intimate relationship, it stands to reason that intimacy cannot take root and flourish in an atmosphere where fear and the threat of punishment exist. In such relationships, protection of the self becomes an overriding concern.

Common Receiver Problems

Receiver problems are caused by a number of factors. The easiest receiver problem to identify and remedy is one that is caused by a physical hearing impairment. In clinical practice, such cases are rare. Usually, receiver problems are more complex and subtle. For example:

1. *Poor attending skills.* Lack of concentration, poor concentration, and distractibility on the receiver's part are frequent causes of misunderstanding and message distortion. When inability to concentrate and distractibility are not the results of a physical condition, poor attending skills may be the cause. However, the inability to concentrate and focus on the message that is being sent may also be symptomatic of the receiver's emotional state (e.g., anxiety, depression, stress, anger).
2. *Defensiveness.* When the message sent is one that the receiver does not wish to hear or when the message sent is one with which the receiver

may disagree, the receiver may actually stop listening to the sender. Frequently, when this occurs, it is because the receiver has become preoccupied with formulating his or her own response to the message. The response may take the form of a rebuttal or counter argument. In cases where the message itself was a hostile or aggressive communication, the receiver may become focused on devising a defensive or counteraggressive retort.

3. *Psychological Factors*. Individuals with certain types of personality disorders and psychiatric conditions may be unable to trust the sender and the message that is sent to them. They may be suspicious of the sender's motives and intentions, they may look for and find hidden meanings in messages, or they may interpret messages in highly distorted, idiosyncratic, or symbolic ways. Some individuals may be unable to hear the message accurately because they are hallucinating or delusional.

It is extremely important, when working with couples, to distinguish between individuals whose suspiciousness, mistrust, attributions of malintention, and so on, stem from past experiences with their partners or whether these receiver difficulties are symptomatic of more serious psychological problems.

Functional communication styles and patterns are a sine qua non for the establishment of intimacy and its continued growth. Therefore, identifying the various causes of communication difficulties that exist in couples' relationships and helping couples correct them (as much as is possible) is the first step in any program in which the goal is the improvement of interpersonal intimacy. Guidelines for helping couples learn how to develop and use functional communication skills appear in Chapter 5, Figures 5.7 and 5.8.

3
CHAPTER

The Intimacy Needs Survey: An Experimental Measure for Clinicians

The dynamic, interactive, reciprocal, and highly subjective nature of intimacy is difficult to measure accurately. At this time, only one empirically developed instrument, the PAIR Inventory (Personal Assessment of Intimacy in Relationships; Shaefer & Olson, 1981) exists. In 1981, these two researchers conducted an empirical investigation designed to assess seven different aspects of intimacy that had been previously identified by Olson (1975, 1977). These seven dimensions were (a) emotional, (b) social, (c) intellectual, (d) sexual, (e) recreational, (f) spiritual, and (g) aesthetic. A factor analytic study was then undertaken by Shaefer and Olson, who administered a 75-item questionnaire to 192 married couples. The 75 items in this initial questionnaire addressed the seven a priori categories of intimacy previously proposed by Olson. Factor analyses produced five statistically significant factor components of intimacy: emotional intimacy, social intimacy, sexual intimacy, intellectual intimacy, and recreational intimacy. Shaefer and Olson (1981) then selected the ten highest loading items contained in each empirically derived factor for inclusion in a 50-item PAIR scale. The current version of PAIR contains only 36 items, 6 items for each of the five dimensions and a 6-item conventionality scale.

PAIR is an easily administered and quickly scored measure that provides the therapist with global ideal/perceived intimacy satisfaction comparison scores for each spouse. Although PAIR does take into account the multidimensional nature of intimacy, it does not deal with the full complexity of the construct—namely, total needs strength, component needs strengths, receptivity satisfaction, and reciprocity satisfaction. Only the Intimacy Needs Survey, mentioned earlier, attempts to measure the dynamic, interactive, reciprocal, and highly subjective nature of intimacy. At this point in time, however, the Intimacy Needs Survey is still in the experimental stages of its development. It cannot, therefore, be considered a scientifically sound, empirically based measure of intimacy and should only be used as a clinical aid by therapists who would like to help couples (a) talk more openly and frankly about their intimate experiences together, (b) learn more about their intimacy needs, (c) identify those areas of their relationship where they are experiencing acceptable levels of need satisfaction, and (d) shed some light on those areas of intimacy where acceptable levels of satisfaction have yet to be achieved. In this chapter, administration, scoring, and interpretation of the Intimacy Needs Survey are discussed.

☐ Administration

Administration of the Intimacy Needs Survey is simple and straight forward. Couples are given the 10-page survey consisting of 40 Likert-type questions. Instructions for completing the survey appear on the cover sheet. The Intimacy Needs Survey and its instructions are reproduced on the following pages.

☐ Scoring

For the first eight subcomponent needs in the Intimacy Needs Survey (i.e., Psychological, Intellectual, Sexual, Spiritual, Aesthetic, Social/Recreational and Physical), numerical scores are computed. The final dimension, Time, is viewed qualitatively and is considered separately. Three scores are computed for each of the eight component needs examined in the survey. These scores include: Component Needs Strengths, Receptivity Satisfaction, and Reciprocity Satisfaction. A Total Intimacy Needs Strength score is calculated simply by summing all eight Component Needs Strengths scores. A sample scoring sheet is presented in Figure 3.1.

Intimacy Needs Survey

Instructions

Intimacy or interpersonal closeness is made up of nine different, yet related, component needs. This questionnaire was developed to help you determine the strength of your need levels in all nine areas and to help you evaluate the extent to which your partner is currently meeting your intimacy needs in each of these nine areas.

In the next few pages, you will be given a definition for each of the nine needs of intimacy. For each need that is described, you are asked to answer a series of questions about yourself and your partner. Please answer each question honestly. Do not omit any questions. All questions must be answered in order for the survey to be scored correctly. There are no "right" or "wrong" answers.

Do not talk with your partner about the survey while you are completing it. You will have ample time to discuss and compare your surveys together with the counselor once they have been scored. If you have any questions please ask the counselor before you begin.

Thank you.

Survey page 1

Emotional Intimacy

Definition – Emotional intimacy is the need for communicating and sharing with your partner all your feelings, both positive (e.g., happiness, joy, elation, gladness, excitement) and negative (e.g., sadness, unhappiness, fear, anger, guilt, shame, loneliness, boredom, fatigue).

(a)   In general, how strong is your need to communicate and share your feelings? (circle only one number).

1   2   3   4   5   6   7   8   9   10

Not A Strong   An Extremely
Need At All   Strong Need

(b)   How important is it for you that your partner be receptive to and listen to you whenever you share your feelings? (circle only one number).

1   2   3   4   5   6   7   8   9   10

Not At All   Extremely
Important   Important

(c)   To what extent is your partner able to meet and satisfy your need for emotional intimacy? (circle only one number).

1   2   3   4   5   6   7   8   9   10

Not At All Able   Totally Satisfies
To Satisfy This Need   This Need

(d)   How important is it for you and your satisfaction with your partner that he or she communicate and share with you his or her positive and negative feelings? (circle only one number).

1   2   3   4   5   6   7   8   9   10

Not At All   Extremely
Important   Important

(e)   To what extent is your partner able to meet and satisfy your expectations for sharing and communicating his or her feelings with you? (circle only one number).

1   2   3   4   5   6   7   8   9   10

Not At All Able   Totally Satisfies
To Satisfy My Expectations   This Expectation

Survey page 2

Psychological Intimacy

Definition – Psychological intimacy is the need to communicate, share, and disclose personal material, information, and feelings about the self to one's partner. Psychological intimacy also includes the need for disclosing and sharing one's hopes, dreams, fantasies, aspirations, and plans for the future as well as sharing one's fears, concerns, and insecurities with one's partner.

(a)   In general, how strong is your need for psychological intimacy? (circle only one number).

1	2	3	4	5	6	7	8	9	10

Not A Strong   An Extremely
Need At All   Strong Need

(b)   How important is it for you that your partner be receptive to and listen to you whenever you disclose intimate details about yourself, your hopes. dreams, problems, concerns, etc.? (circle only one number).

1	2	3	4	5	6	7	8	9	10

Not At All   Extremely
Important   Important

(c)   To what extent is your partner able to meet and satisfy your need for psychological intimacy? (circle only one number).

1	2	3	4	5	6	7	8	9	10

Not At All Able   Totally Satisfies
To Satisfy This Need   This Need

(d)   How important is it for you and your satisfaction with your partner that he or she communicate, share and disclose to you information and details about himself or herself and that he or she share his or her innermost fears, concerns, problems, hopes, dreams, desires, etc., with you? (circle only one number).

1	2	3	4	5	6	7	8	9	10

Not At All   Extremely
Important   Important

(e)   To what extent is your partner able to meet and satisfy your expectations for disclosing information about himself or herself and sharing with you his or her innermost fears, concerns, problems, hopes, dreams, desires, etc.? (circleonly one number).

1	2	3	4	5	6	7	8	9	10

Not At All Able   Totally Satisfies
To Satisfy My Expectations   This Expectation

Survey page 3

Intellectual Intimacy

Definition – Intellectual intimacy is the need to communicate and share important ideas, thoughts, beliefs, etc., with your partner.

(a) In general, how strong is your need to communicate and share ideas thoughts, beliefs, etc., that are important to you with your partner? (circle only one number).

1	2	3	4	5	6	7	8	9	10

Not A Strong   An Extremely
Need At All   Strong Need

(b) How important is it for you that your partner listen to you whenever you share ideas, thoughts, beliefs, etc. that are important to you? (circle only one number).

1	2	3	4	5	6	7	8	9	10

Not At All   Extremely
Important   Important

(c) To what extent is your partner able to meet and satisfy your need for intellectual intimacy? (circle only one number).

1	2	3	4	5	6	7	8	9	10

Not At All Able   Totally Satisfies
To Satisfy This Need   This Need

(d) How important is it for you and your satisfaction with your partner that he or she communicate and share with you his or her ideas, thoughts, beliefs, etc.? (circle only one number).

1	2	3	4	5	6	7	8	9	10

Not At All   Extremely
Important   Important

(e) To what extent is your partner able to meet and satisfy your expectations for sharing and communicating his or her ideas, thoughts, beliefs, etc.? (circle only one number).

1	2	3	4	5	6	7	8	9	10

Not At All Able   Totally Satisfies
To Satisfy My Expectations   This Expectation

Survey page 4

Sexual Intimacy

Definition – Sexual intimacy is the need for communicating, sharing, and expressing thoughts, feelings, desires, and fantasies that are of a sexual nature. Sexual intimacy includes sharing erotic experiences together (e.g., watching erotic films, listening to erotic music, reading erotic material, etc.). Sexual intimacy also includes the need for physical closeness, body contact, involvement, and interactions that are specifically designed to be sexually arousing, stimulating, exciting, and satisfying (e.g., erotic kissing, petting, hugging, dancing, fondling, bathing). Sexually intimate behavior may or may not lead to sexual intercourse and/or orgasm for one or both parties involved.

(a)   In general, how strong is your need for sexual intimacy? (circle only one number).

1	2	3	4	5	6	7	8	9	10

Not A Strong   An Extremely
Need At All   Strong Need

(b)   How important is it for you that your partner be receptive to you whenever you share your thoughts, feelings, desires, etc., about sexual matters? (circle only one number).

1	2	3	4	5	6	7	8	9	10

Not At All   Extremely
Important   Important

(c)   To what extent is your partner able to meet and satisfy your need for sexual intimacy? (circle only one number).

1	2	3	4	5	6	7	8	9	10

Not At All Able   Totally Satisfies
To Satisfy This Need   This Need

(d)   How important is it for you that your partner share with you his or her sexual thoughts, feelings, desires, and fantasies and communicates his or her sexual needs to you? (circle only one number).

1	2	3	4	5	6	7	8	9	10

Not At All   Extremely
Important   Important

(e)   To what extent is your partner able to meet and satisfy your expectations for sharing his or her sexual thoughts, feelings, needs, desires, etc.? (circle only one number).

1	2	3	4	5	6	7	8	9	10

Not At All Able   Totally Satisfies
To Satisfy My Expectations   This Expectation

Physical (Nonsexual) Intimacy

Definition – Physical intimacy is the need for physical closeness and body contact with one's partner. Physical closeness includes such experiences as holding hands, cuddling together, slow dancing with one's partner, nonsexual touching (e.g., patting, caressing, hugging), kissing that is not a prelude to sexual relations, sleeping in the same bed with one's partner, walking together arm-in-arm, etc.

(a)   In general, how strong is your need for physical (nonsexual) intimacy? (circle only one number).

1	2	3	4	5	6	7	8	9	10

Not A Strong   An Extremely
Need At All   Strong Need

(b)   How important is it for you for your partner to be receptive to physical (nonsexual) advances that you initiate? (circle only one number).

1	2	3	4	5	6	7	8	9	10

Not At All Important   Extremely Important

(c)   To what extent is your partner able to meet and satisfy your need for physical (nonsexual) closeness and contact? (circle only one number).

1	2	3	4	5	6	7	8	9	10

Not At All Able   Totally Satisfies
To Satisfy This Need   This Need

(d)   How important is it for you for your partner to initiate physical (nonsexual) closeness and contact? (circle only one number).

1	2	3	4	5	6	7	8	9	10

Not At All Important   Extremely Important

(e)   To what extent is your partner able to meet and satisfy your expectations for initiating physical (nonsexual) contact with you? (circle only one number).

1	2	3	4	5	6	7	8	9	10

Not At All Able   Totally Satisfies
To Satisfy My Expectations   This Expectation

Survey page 6

Spiritual Intimacy

Definition – Spiritual intimacy is the need to share one's thoughts, feelings, beliefs, and experiences with one's partner that have to do with religion, the supernatural, moral values, the meaning of existence, life after death, one's relationship to God, etc. Spiritual intimacy also includes the joint practice and participation together with one's partner in religious activities, rituals, celebrations, experiences, etc. Spiritual intimacy between two people does not necessarily require that they share the same religion.

(a)   In general, how strong is your need for spiritual intimacy? (circle only one number).

1   2   3   4   5   6   7   8   9   10

Not A Strong   An Extremely
Need At All   Strong Need

(b)   How important is it for you that your partner be receptive to and listen to you when you share and communicate your thoughts, feelings, beliefs and experiences about spiritual issues? (circle only one number).

1   2   3   4   5   6   7   8   9   10

Not At All Important   Extremely Important

(c)   To what extent is your partner able to meet and satisfy your need for spiritual intimacy? (circle only one number).

1   2   3   4   5   6   7   8   9   10

Not At All Able   Totally Satisfies
To Satisfy This Need   This Need

(d)   How important is it for you and your satisfaction with your partner that he or she communicate and share his or her spiritual thoughts, beliefs, feelings and experiences with you? (circle only one number).

1   2   3   4   5   6   7   8   9   10

Not At All Important   Extremely Important

(e)   How important is it for you that you and your partner participate together in religious activities, rituals, celebrations, experiences, etc.? (circle only one number).

1   2   3   4   5   6   7   8   9   10

Not At All Important   Extremely Important

(f)   To what extent is your partner able to satisfy your expectations for communicating and sharing his or her spiritual thoughts, beliefs, experiences, etc.? (circle only one number).

1   2   3   4   5   6   7   8   9   10

Not At All Able   Totally Satisfies
To Satisfy My Expectations   This Expectation

Survey page 7

Aesthetic Intimacy

Definition – Aesthetic intimacy is the need and desire to share with one's partner feelings and experiences that are considered to be beautiful, breathtaking, or awe inspiring, such as the wonders of nature and the cosmos, music, art, poetry, literature, etc.

(a)   In general, how strong is your need and desire for aesthetic sharing? (circle only one number).

1   2   3   4   5   6   7   8   9   10

Not A Strong   An Extremely
Need At All   Strong Need

(b)   How important is it for you that your partner listen to you whenever you attempt to communicate and share aesthetic feelings and experiences with him or her? (circle only one number).

1   2   3   4   5   6   7   8   9   10

Not At All Important   Extremely Important

(c)   To what extent is your partner able to meet and satisfy your need for aesthetic intimacy? (circle only one number).

1   2   3   4   5   6   7   8   9   10

Not At All Able   Totally Satisfies
To Satisfy This Need   This Need

(d)   How important is it for you and your satisfaction with your partner that he or she share with you experiences and feelings that he or she considers to be beautiful, breathtaking, or awe inspiring? (circle only one number).

1   2   3   4   5   6   7   8   9   10

Not At All Important   Extremely Important

(e)   To what extent is your partner able to meet and satisfy your expectations for communicating and sharing with you experiences and feelings that he or she considers to be beautiful, breathtaking, and awe inspiring? (circle only one number).

1   2   3   4   5   6   7   8   9   10

Not At All Able   Totally Satisfies
To Satisfy My Expectations   This Expectation

Survey page 8

Social and Recreational Intimacy

Definition – Social and recreational intimacy is the need to engage in playful and enjoyable activities and experiences with one's partner. Social and recreational intimacy includes activities and experiences such as exchanging jokes and humorous stories; sharing one's daily experiences and discussing daily events with one's partner; sharing meals, snacks, and refreshments with one's partner; exercising together; playing sports and games together; sharing hobbies; dancing together for pleasure and enjoyment; vacationing together; etc.

(a)   In general, how strong is your need for social and recreational intimacy? (circle only one number).

| 1 | 2 | 3 | 4 | 5 | 6 | 7 | 8 | 9 | 10 |

Not A Strong   An Extremely
Need At All   Strong Need

(b)   How important is it for you that your partner engage in social and recreational activities with you that you initiate? (circle only one number).

| 1 | 2 | 3 | 4 | 5 | 6 | 7 | 8 | 9 | 10 |

Not At All Important   Extremely Important

(c)   To what extent is your partner able to meet and satisfy your need for social and recreational intimacy? (circle only one number).

| 1 | 2 | 3 | 4 | 5 | 6 | 7 | 8 | 9 | 10 |

Not At All Able   Totally Satisfies
To Satisfy This Need   This Need

(d)   How important is it for you that your partner initiate and ask you to participate in social and recreational activities with him or her? (circle only one number).

| 1 | 2 | 3 | 4 | 5 | 6 | 7 | 8 | 9 | 10 |

Not At All Important   Extremely Important

(e)   To what extent is your partner able to meet and satisfy your expectations for initiating and involving you in social and recreational activities with him or her? (circle only one number).

| 1 | 2 | 3 | 4 | 5 | 6 | 7 | 8 | 9 | 10 |

Not At All Able   Totally Satisfies
To Satisfy My Expectations   This Expectation

Survey page 9

Temporal Intimacy

The final dimension of intimacy—Time—is assessed by the following three questions:

Consider the amount of time, on a daily basis, that you spend together with your partner.

1.   Does the amount of time you currently spend with your partner allow you to have the intimacy you would like to have in your relationship?

Yes_____   No_____

2.   What is the minimum amount of time, on a daily basis, that you require in order for you to feel intimately related to your partner?

Hours_____   Minutes_____

3.   How much time, on a daily basis, do you think you would have to spend together with your partner for you to feel that your needs for intimacy were being met satisfactorily?

Hours_____   Minutes_____

☐ INTERPRETATION

Once a couple's Intimacy Needs Survey scores have been computed, they are transferred to a Summary Sheet. This sheet is used to provide feedback to the couple. Partners' scores are juxtaposed on the Summary Sheet so that comparisons of the various scores can be made. The Summary Sheet has four sections. The first section compares Component Needs Strength scores and Total Needs Strength scores. The second section addresses each partner's satisfaction with his or her mate's acceptance, responsiveness, and openness to the expression of need in the first eight areas of intimacy. These eight scores are called Receptivity Satisfaction scores. Section three deals with each partner's satisfaction with his or her mate's depth levels of reciprocal sharing and self-disclosure in these same eight areas of intimacy. These scores are called Reciprocity Satisfaction scores. Finally, in the fourth section, couples can compare their time needs for intimacy. A Summary Sheet is reproduced as Figure 3.2.

I   Emotional Intimacy
     Need Strength   = (a) ___ × ___ (b) = ___ (1)   I._____
     Satisfaction   = (c) ___ × ___ (b) = ___ (2)
     Need Strength/Satisfaction Index is (2) or (_) = ___ = Receptive to me ___%
                                (1)   (_)
     Reciprocity Expectation Satisfaction is (e) or (_) = ___ = Shares with me ___%
                                  (d)   (_)

II   Psychological Intimacy
     Need Strength   = (a) ___ × ___ (b) = ___ (1)   I._____
     Satisfaction   = (c) ___ × ___ (b) = ___ (2)
     Need Strength/Satisfaction Index is (2) or (_) = ___ = Receptive to me ___%
                                  (1)   (_)
     Reciprocity Expectation Satisfaction is (e) or (_) = ___ = Shares with me ___%
                                  (d)   (_)

III   Intellectual Intimacy
     Need Strength   = (a) ___ × ___ (b) = ___ (1)   I._____
     Satisfaction   = (c) ___ × ___ (b) = ___ (2)
     Need Strength/Satisfaction Index is (2) or (_) = ___ = Receptive to me ___%
                                  (1)   (_)
     Reciprocity Expectation Satisfaction is (e) or (_) = ___ = Shares with me ___%
                                  (d)   (_)

IV   Sexual Intimacy
     Need Strength   = (a) ___ × ___ (b) = ___ (1)   I._____
     Satisfaction   = (c) ___ × ___ (b) = ___ (2)
     Need Strength/Satisfaction Index is (2) or (_) = ___ = Receptive to me ___%
                                  (1)   (_)
     Reciprocity Expectation Satisfaction is (e) or (_) = ___ = Shares with me ___%
                                  (d)   (_)

V   Spritual Intimacy
     Need Strength   = (a) ___ × ___ (b) = ___ (1)   I._____
     Satisfaction   = (c) ___ × ___ (b) = ___ (2)
     Need Strength/Satisfaction Index is (2) or (_) = ___ = Receptive to me ___%
                                  (1)   (_)
     Reciprocity Expectation Satisfaction is (f) or (_) = ___ = Shares with me ___%
                                  (d)   (_)

Continued

FIGURE 3.1. Intimacy Needs Survey Score Sheet

VI Aesthetic Intimacy
    Need Strength = (a) ___ × ___ (b) = ___ (1)   I._____
    Satisfaction   = (c) ___ × ___ (b) = ___ (2)
    Need Strength/Satisfaction Index is (2) or (_) = ___ = Receptive to me ___%
                    (1)   (_)
    Reciprocity Expectation Satisfaction is (e) or (_) = ___ = Shares with me ___%
                    (d)   (_)

VII Social and Recreational Intimacy
    Need Strength = (a) ___ × ___ (b) = ___ (1)   I._____
    Satisfaction   = (c) ___ × ___ (b) = ___ (2)
    Need Strength/Satisfaction Index is (2) or (_) = ___ = Receptive to me ___%
                    (1)   (_)
    Reciprocity Expectation Satisfaction is (e) or (_) = ___ = Shares with me ___%
                    (d)   (_)

VIII Physical Intimacy
    Need Strength = (a) ___ × ___ (b) = ___ (1)   I._____
    Satisfaction   = (c) ___ × ___ (b) = ___ (2)
    Need Strength/Satisfaction Index is (2) or (_) = ___ = Receptive to me ___%
                    (1)   (_)
    Reciprocity Expectation Satisfaction is (e) or (_) = ___ = Shares with me ___%
                    (d)   (_)

IX Time Needs
    1. Satisfaction   Yes___   No___
    2. Minimum time Hours ___   Minutes ___
    3. Desired time   Hours ___   Minutes ___

FIGURE 3.1. Intimacy Needs Survey Score Sheet

Section I			Section II			Section III			Section IV	
Component Needs Strengths			Receptivity Satisfaction			Reciprocity Satisfaction			Time Satisfaction	
	H	W		H	W		H	W		Satisfaction Now
I Emotional									H	Yes ___ No ___
II Psychological									W	Yes ___ No ___
III Intellectual										Minimum Time
IV Sexual										Hours Minutes
V Spiritual									H	___ ___
VI Aesthetic									W	___ ___
VII Social/Recreational										Desired Time
VIII Physical										Hours Minutes
									H	___ ___
Total Needs Score	___	___							W	___ ___
Comments			Comments			Comments			Comments	

FIGURE 3.2. Intimacy Needs Survey Summary Sheet

4

CHAPTER

Assessment Considerations

☐ Overview

- Assessments
- Individual considerations
- Couple considerations
- Case illustration: Fiona and Paul
- Marital types: The Spousal Inventory of Desired Changes and Relationship Barriers (SIDCARB)
- Four steps in the assessment process

The Intimacy Needs Survey can be used in work with individuals as well as with couples. With individual clients, it can be administered independently or incorporated into a more comprehensive test battery. With couples, the Intimacy Needs Survey is best used in conjunction with other measures of marital dynamics to provide a more rounded, complete, and multidimensional view of the relationship (Bagarozzi, 1989; L'Abate & Bagarozzi, 1993).

☐ Individual Psychotherapy

Frequently, clients enter psychotherapy because of a failed relationship or after a series of failed relationships. When this is the presenting problem, it is helpful to take a thorough and detailed history of the client's intimate relationships in order to determine if, indeed, difficulties with intimacy have been primarily responsible for these failed relationships. In other instances, clients may present for therapy with concerns about intimacy being their chief complaint. In such cases, the client may identify the problem as one of having difficulties with "closeness" or "commitment." In other cases, the client may express fears of revealing his or her "true self" or of expressing his or her "innermost feelings."

Difficulties with intimacy often are presented as sexual problems in failed relationships. When sexual concerns and dysfunctions that do not have a medical cause or component are said to have been responsible for relationship failures, problems with intimacy should be explored as part of any sex history that is taken by the therapist (Masters & Johnson, 1970).

Sometimes, however, a client may have become aware of intimacy as a problematic issue in a failed relationship only after his or her partner identified it as a cause for concern and reason for terminating the relationship.

In all these cases, the Intimacy Needs Survey can be administered to the client (using the most recent previous partner as a reference) to help him or her become aware of the actual strengths of his or her needs. Once Total Needs Strength and Component Needs Strengths scores have been calculated, a clearer picture of relationship difficulties in this area will emerge. For example, assessment may reveal that the client's Total Needs Strength score is extremely high and that very few people would be able to satisfy such a strong need for intimacy. Conversely, Intimacy Needs Survey results may show that the client's needs for intimacy in all component areas are very low, and consequently, his or her Total Needs Strength score is extremely low. Here, the client faces a different reality, namely, that even a spouse or partner whose needs for intimacy fall within normal limits might still feel unconnected, unfulfilled, and dissatisfied with such low levels of intimate exchanges.

Typically, when one partner's needs are extreme, his or her significant other feels uncomfortable and frustrated. Spouses and partners of extremely high-needs individuals often experience them as needy, clinging, demanding, controlling, and so on, while partners of extremely low-needs individuals often experience them as cold, aloof, distant, withholding, rejecting, and the like.

When the Intimacy Needs Survey scores for a client are found to be within normal limits, some type of intimacy needs discrepancy should be suspected as contributing to relationship failure. In such instances, Reciprocity and Receptivity dissatisfaction scores can be very informative in helping to identify possible areas of needs discrepancies.

Sometimes individuals seek professional consultation in order to help them make a decision about intimate relationships in which they are involved. For instance, a client may be having difficulty choosing between two (and sometimes among three) prospective partners. In some cases, the client may be considering whether to remain in a relationship with a current partner, or whether to leave that person for someone who might be able to satisfy his or her intimacy needs more fully. Having these clients complete the Intimacy Needs Survey for each person who is the source of uncertainty can be enlightening (Bagarozzi, 1999).

☐ Couples Assessment

The Intimacy Needs Survey can be used with couples in a wide variety of settings—specifically, educational, enrichment and clinical. For example, therapists who engage in premarital education, counseling, and preparation can make use of the Intimacy Needs Survey to help couples explore and assess this area of their relationship. In Chapter 2, we saw how Mike and Jane completed the Intimacy Needs Survey as part of a hierarchically sequenced program of premarital education and training developed by the author (Bagarozzi, 1986; Bagarozzi & Bagarozzi, 1982; Bagarozzi, Bagarozzi, Anderson, & Pollane, 1984). The reader will recall that Mike and Jane's Total Intimacy Needs Strengths scores were not very different. However, their Component Needs Strengths scores, in certain critical areas for Jane, differed considerably. When significant needs discrepancies are discovered for individuals contemplating marriage, the therapist must be able to interpret Intimacy Needs Survey scores to the couple in a way that will enable them to make an informed decision about the future of their relationship.

Recommendations to terminate the relationship or to reconsider the decision to marry when serious needs discrepancies and significant dissatisfactions are found should be avoided by the therapist even though marital compatibility in this area of the couple's relationship appears to be problematic. Such important decisions are best left to the couple. The therapist must keep in mind that intimacy, although an important factor in most marriages, represents only one aspect of marital satisfaction and may play only a small role in maintaining marital stability (Bagarozzi, 1983; Bagarozzi & Pollane, 1983; Bagarozzi & Wodarski, 1977). To illustrate this point, the following case is presented.

Several years ago, Fiona and Paul came to see the author for premarital counseling. Fiona was a strikingly beautiful woman whose looks were matched only by her intelligence. She held a masters degree in music and played first chair violin in a large metropolitan city orchestra. She was outgoing, assertive, and self-confident. She had been dating Paul for almost a year.

Paul was a soft-spoken veterinarian who described himself as someone who was more comfortable with animals than with people. Paul had been married previously to a woman who, tragically, died shortly after the birth of their daughter, Molly. After his wife's death, Paul devoted himself to raising Molly. When he was not engaged in his veterinary practice, he was with Molly. Paul began to date again only after Molly entered elementary school. None of these dating relationships was felt to be significant until Paul met Fiona.

Paul's and Fiona's needs for intimacy differed considerably, as can be seen from their Intimacy Needs Survey scores shown in Figure 4.1 on the following page.

Total Intimacy Needs Survey scores have been found to average between 450 and 600, the range being 10 to 800. Paul's score of 430 placed him in the Low Average category. Fiona's Total Intimacy Needs Survey score of 670, on the other hand, placed her in the High score category. No discrepancy scores below 70% were found for either Paul or Fiona in the area of Receptivity satisfaction. The only problematic dimension was Reciprocity satisfaction from Fiona's perspective. Five areas of intimacy were identified as falling below acceptable levels of satisfaction: Emotional, Psychological, Intellectual, Spiritual, and Aesthetic. Nevertheless, Fiona chose to marry Paul in spite of these clearly identified dissatisfactions in needs areas that she considered to be very important to her and central to her identity. Why, then, the reader might ask, did Fiona elect to marry Paul? The answer to this question lies outside the realm of intimacy. To understand Fiona's decision, some information from her intimate relationship history will be helpful.

Prior to meeting Paul, Fiona had lived with a man for several years. Like herself, he was an artist, a painter of some repute. Fiona described their relationship as stormy and passionate. During the "good times" they were "soul mates" who "connected deeply" in all those areas of intimacy that were important to her, namely, Emotional, Psychological, Intellectual, Sexual, Spiritual, and Aesthetic. However, he was unable to commit to marriage or to any type of long-term relationship. Furthermore, he had no interest in ever having children. After a long period of self-exploration and psychotherapy, Fiona decided that it was best for her and for her future to end their relationship. She wanted something more "stable" and "permanent." Most of all, she wanted to have children.

Shortly after Fiona moved to her own apartment, she found a stray kitten whom she named Fred. A friend suggested that she take Fred to Paul, who was her friend's veterinarian. When Fiona arrived at Paul's office, he was talking to his daughter, Molly. Fiona was taken by Paul's relationship with Molly. She was attracted to his kindness and his strong, yet gentle, manner. It was apparent to her that Paul was a loving and caring father. After several visits to Paul's office with Fred, Fiona invited Paul to dinner. Paul accepted, and they began to date steadily. The more

Section I			Section II			Section III			Section IV
Component Needs Strengths			Receptivity Satisfaction			Reciprocity Satisfaction			Time Satisfaction
	Paul	Fiona		Paul	Fiona		Paul	Fiona	Satisfaction Now
I Emotional	60	90		100%	100%		100%	60%	P Yes X No __
II Psychological	60	90		100%	100%		100%	60%	F Yes X No __
III Intellectual	70	90		100%	100%		100%	40%	Minimum Time
IV Sexual	90	90		100%	100%		100%	100%	Hours Minutes
V Spiritual	20	80		100%	80%		100%	60%	P 1 __
VI Aesthetic	40	100		100%	80%		100%	50%	F 1 __
VII Social/Recreational	40	60		100%	100%		100%	100%	Desired Time
VIII Physical	50	70		100%	100%		100%	100%	Hours Minutes
Total Needs Score	430	670							P 1 __
									F 1 __
Comments			Comments			Comments			Comments
Paul's score – Low Average Fiona's score – High			No discrepancies in Receptivity Satisfaction for Paul or Fiona.			Paul is satisfied with the Reciprocity dimension. Fiona is dissatisfied in 5 areas of Receptivity.			

FIGURE 4.1. Intimacy Needs Survey Summary Sheet for Paul and Fiona.

time Fiona spent with Paul, the more she appreciated him, his strength of character, and his sincerity. After several months of exclusive dating, she and Paul began to discuss the possibility of marriage and children.

Fiona was not surprised by the discrepancies between her scores and Paul's that were found once their Intimacy Needs Surveys had been scored. As part of the premarital counseling process, they discussed their needs differences and developed a workable solution that would enable Fiona to satisfy her unfulfilled needs for Emotional, Psychological, Intellectual, and Aesthetic intimacy through relationships with her friends. She was able to bring a spiritual dimension to her relationship with Paul and Molly, and this she found to be very fulfilling. In addition, Molly's interest in theater and dance also helped Fiona meet some of her Aesthetic needs.

☐ Marital Therapy: Basic Considerations

Marital relationships can be classified according to three ideal types (Bagarozzi & Wodarski, 1977). These are described below:

Type I: Mutually Rewarding and Satisfying Marriages
When both husband and wife are free to terminate the marriage at any time, marital stability and cohesion are maintained only because both spouses are satisfied with the type of social exchange system that currently governs their relationship (intimacy being a form of socio-emotional exchange), and neither spouse perceives a more attractive alternative to be available. Such marriages are considered to be *voluntary marriages.*

Type II: Unsatisfying Marriages with No Better Alternatives Available
Spouses involved in unsatisfying and unfulfilling relationships (in which social exchange inequities and punishments characterize the marriage), will continue in these relationships only until a more viable and satisfying alternative is perceived. Such marriages are considered to be *unstable marriages.*

Type III: Nonvoluntary Marriages
When spouses feel compelled to stay in an unsatisfying or punishing relationship, because they perceive insurmountable barriers to separation and divorce, the marriage is considered to be *nonvoluntary.*

Before using the Intimacy Needs Survey in work with distressed marriages, it is helpful for the therapist to know how each spouse perceives the marriage, since Intimacy Needs Survey scores are best understood and interpreted when they are considered within the broader context of a couple's overall relationship dynamics. The Spousal Inventory of Desired Changes and Relationship Barriers (SIDCARB[1]; Bagarozzi, 1983; Bagarozzi & Atilano, 1982; Bagarozzi & Pollane, 1983) was developed to help therapists gain a multidimensional view of marriage as conceptualized by social exchange theorists (Adams, 1963, 1965; Blood & Wolfe, 1960; Carson, 1969; Edwards, 1969; Foa, 1971; Homans, 1974; Levinger, 1976; Thibaut & Kelley, 1959; Waller & Hill, 1951). SIDCARB operationalized the major theoretical constructs of social exchange theory as applied to marriages. These are:

1. Each spouse's satisfaction with his or her partner and the marriage in 10 areas of the relationship. Satisfaction is based upon the spouses' subjective evaluation of the fairness of social exchanges in these 10 areas.
2. The amount of change desired in a partner's behavior in each of these 10 areas of the marriage.
3. The strength of the relationship barriers perceived by each spouse when the marriage is experienced as dissatisfying.
4. Marital power as conceptualized according to the principle of least interest (Waller & Hill, 1951), namely, the more powerful spouse is the spouse who has less to lose by terminating the marriage. Essentially, the spouse who perceives fewer, lower, or weaker barriers to separation and divorce is the spouse who possesses relatively more power in the marriage.

According to the social exchange model of marriage, a spouse can perceive his or her relationship to his or her mate in nine possible ways when three levels of marital satisfaction and three levels of barrier strength are considered together, as illustrated in Figure 4.2.

The therapist using SIDCARB must consider how both spouses perceive their marriage before attempting to interpret Intimacy Needs Survey scores and giving the couple feedback. Figure 4.3 shows all possible combinations of two spouses' perceptions of the same marriage when three levels of satisfaction and three levels of barrier strength are considered together.

SIDCARB data provide the therapist with valuable information about satisfactions and barrier strengths, thereby operationalizing the principle of least interest and relative marital power. Information about a couple's power dynamics is best left undisclosed and uninterpreted. This information, however, allows the therapist to understand Intimacy Needs Survey scores within a larger relationship context of relational power dynamics.

---

[1]The Spousal Inventory of Desired Changes and Relationship Barriers (SIDCARB) and scoring guidelines appear in Appendix A.

SATISFACTION

	High	Medium	Low
Low	1 L/H	2 L/M	3 L/L
<u>BARRIERS</u> Medium	4 M/H	5 M/M	6 M/L
High	7 H/H	8 H/M	9 H/L

FIGURE 4.2. A spouse's possible perceptions of his or her marriage when three levels of barriers and three levels of satisfaction are considered together.

The degree to which intimacy can be increased or enhanced in a couple's relationship depends upon several factors which the therapist must take into account before a couple-specific intervention program can be developed. Each couple should be evaluated separately. The following assessment procedure is suggested.

1. *Assess the couple's relationship dynamics.* The type of relationship presented by the couple must first be evaluated. Each spouse's satisfaction with his or her partner and the marriage, each spouse's perception of barriers to separation and divorce, and the power dynamics of the marriage must be considered. The therapist may wish to consider which combination of couple's perception of marriage (as shown in Figure 4.3) best represents a given couple's relationship.

   It is important to remember that marital satisfaction, barriers to relationship dissolution, and power arrangements are dynamic processes that change with the passage of time, the stage of the marriage and family life cycle, and the evolution of the relationship. These perceptions represent only the current state of marital dynamics.

2. *Assess Intimacy Needs Strengths, identify discrepancies and locate dissatisfactions.* The extent to which Total Intimacy Needs Strength scores differ between partners must be assessed and understood by the therapist.

FIGURE 4.3. (opposite) A comparison of a husband and wife's possible perceptions of their marriage when three levels of satisfaction and three levels of barrier strength are considered. L = Low; M = Medium; H = High; B = Barrier Strength; S = Satisfaction.

Husband's Perceptions-Barriers and Satisfaction

Wife ↓ \ Husband →	HB/LS	HB/MS	HB/HS	MB/LS	MB/MS	MB/HS	LB/LS	LB/MS	LB/HS
LB/HS	9	8	7	6	5	4	3	2	1
LB/MS	18	17	16	15	14	13	12	11	10
LB/LS	27	26	25	24	23	22	21	20	19
MB/HS	36	35	34	33	32	31	30	29	28
MB/MS	45	44	43	42	41	40	39	38	37
MB/LS	54	53	52	51	50	49	48	47	46
HB/HS	63	62	61	60	59	58	57	56	55
HB/MS	72	71	70	69	68	67	66	65	64
HB/LS	81	80	79	78	77	76	75	74	73

Wife's Perceptions-Barriers and Satisfaction

53

Since intimacy needs strengths are thought to be fairly stable and trait-like, an accurate appraisal of them must be made before realistic and achievable treatment goals can be set.

The first step in achieving this understanding is to identify what factors account for the observed differences in Total Intimacy Needs Strengths scores. For example, do these differences reflect extremely high or extremely low Total Needs Strength scores for one or both spouses? If extreme scores are found to account for these differences, then the therapist will have to help the couple explore the possible ramifications that such differences might have for the future of their relationship, given that intimacy needs strengths may not change very much over the course of one's lifetime.

If extreme scores are not found to be an issue, but significant differences in Total Intimacy Needs Strengths scores are found, a Component Needs Strengths assessment is the next step. To illustrate how to conduct a Component Needs Strengths assessment, let us take the example of a hypothetical couple entering counseling for help with improving the intimacy they share in their marriage. Both spouses perceive their marriage as voluntary with low barriers to relationship termination (LB). The wife's satisfaction level with her marriage is scored as medium (MS); the husband's level of satisfaction is rated high (HS; see box #10 in Figure 4.3). Both spouses' Total Intimacy Needs Strengths scores fall within normal limits. The husband's Total Intimacy Needs Strength score was 480, the wife's, 590.

The first thing that the therapist must identify is whether this 110-point difference represents a relatively small difference in all Component Needs Strength scores or whether this difference is accounted for by a few Component Needs scores where large differences exist. Once this has been determined, the importance of these differences for each spouse's satisfaction can be ascertained by reviewing each spouse's responses to questions (b) and (d) for each Component Need. Pie chart drawings can also be used to help the therapist appreciate the significance and centrality of Component Needs strengths differences for both spouses.

Evaluating Receptivity and Reciprocity Satisfactions is the next task. Essentially, satisfaction in these two areas is the crux of the issue. At this level of analysis, Total Intimacy Needs Strengths differences may not pose a serious problem if the spouse with stronger Component Needs Strengths is experiencing relatively high levels of satisfaction. All that may be required to increase her intimacy satisfaction levels would be for her husband to increase Reciprocity and/or Receptivity, depending upon her needs. However, if Receptivity and/or Reciprocity satisfaction levels are extremely low, the therapist is faced with a more difficult clinical task.

3. *Consider the couple's expectations for change given the degree of marital dissatisfaction present in the relationship.* The more both spouses perceive their marriage as being nonvoluntary and dissatisfying, the more important it is for the therapist to determine how much of the couple's dissatisfaction can be attributed to intimacy problems and differences. There are a number of empirically derived instruments, including SIDCARB, that can be used to help the therapist make this determination (L'Abate & Bagarozzi, 1993). When assessment highlights other areas of marital conflict, the therapist must consider the degree to which these other areas of marital distress might have had a lasting impact upon the couple's ability to become more intimate. When these additional factors are taken into account, the therapist must also consider whether each spouse's expectations for therapeutic outcomes are realistic, given the history, number, and severity of relationship conflicts and each spouse's individual needs strengths and capacities. Helping couples set realistic and achievable treatment goals before counseling is begun is essential if intervention is to be successful.

4. *Assessing relationship skills and interpersonal competencies.* Successful and satisfying marriages can be thought of as resting upon a multileveled foundation of relationship skills with functional communication between spouses serving as the most fundamental skills level. The next level of skills is the couple's ability to negotiate its differences and resolve conflicts in ways that are considered to be fair and equitable by both spouses. The third level of skills making up this foundation has two components: joint problem-solving abilities and decision-making capacities. The ability to set realistic relationship goals and the ability to develop workable plans to achieve these goals constitute the final level of skills necessary for marital success.

There are a number of behavioral tasks that can be assigned to couples which can help the therapist evaluate the extent to which they possess each of these four foundation skills (L'Abate & Bagarozzi, 1993). Some of these will be discussed as examples in the next chapter.

PRACTICAL ISSUES

Practice and Procedures for Enhancing Intimacy: A Case Study of Clara and Ralph

☐ Overview

- The Enhancing Intimacy Program: Overview
- Case example: Clara and Ralph
- Summaries of Clara's and Ralph's intimate relationship histories
- The dynamics of courtship with special attention given to ideal spouse/perceived spouse discrepancies and the cognitive matching process
- Communications assessment guidelines
- Problem identification, decision making, goal setting and planning assessment guidelines
- Conflict negotiation assessment guidelines
- Strategies for offering constructive feedback to couples: Information sharing as an induction process
- Reducing perceived spouse/ideal spouse discrepancies
- Guidelines for developing functional communication skills

The Enhancing Intimacy Program developed by the author and described in this and following chapters has been used for educational and enrichment purposes with couples who do not have long-standing, severe, and numerous conflicts and problems. However, it can be used in conjunction with other more intensive psychotherapeutic approaches that have been developed to treat seriously distressed relationships. The decision to incorporate the Enhancing Intimacy Program as part of a larger intervention program designed to help seriously distressed relationships is a judgment call that can only be made by a therapist who knows the couple well. Before attempting to use this program with a severely distressed couple, the therapist must consider whether the couple will agree (a) to engage in an assessment process consisting of individual interviews designed to gather intimate relationship histories, (b) to complete the Intimacy Needs Survey and the SIDCARB, and (c) to engage in specific behavioral task assignments designed to help the therapist assess communication patterns, conflict negotiation competencies, and problem-solving abilities. In addition, the therapist must consider whether the couple will be able to function within an educational and training format which requires them to learn new skills, practice these skills, and complete homework assignments between sessions.

The Enhancing Intimacy Program begins with an orientation session wherein the importance of accurate preprogram assessment is explained to the couple. Accurate preprogram assessment accomplishes the following:

1. Enables the therapist to work with the couple to develop realistic treatment goals;
2. Allows the therapist to design an intervention program that is specifically tailored to meet the unique needs of the couple;
3. Makes it possible for the therapist to determine the success of the program upon completion by conducting postprogram evaluations.

Next, the rationale for teaching specific skills is presented, and the importance of completing homework assignments is explained. The following points are stressed:

1. The research regarding marital interaction and marital satisfaction is very clear. Couples who have developed functional communication patterns have more satisfying marriages than couples who have not developed such patterns.
2. Functional communication patterns, by themselves, are not sufficient to insure continued marital satisfaction and success. For marital satisfaction to be maintained, couples must learn how to problem solve and negotiate conflicts effectively.
3. In order to increase the probability that the skills learned as part of the program (e.g., communication, problem solving, conflict negotiation) are maintained after formal training has ended, couples must be willing to practice these skills at home and to complete homework assignments designed specifically for them by the therapist.

After these points made by the therapist and discussed with the couple,

I.   Assessments
      (a) Individual interviews
      (b) Intimacy Needs Survey and SIDCARB
      (c) Behavioral interaction tasks
II.   Review of assessment findings
III. Communication, problem solving, and conflict negotiation training
IV.   Addressing needs strengths differences and dealing with needs
      strengths discrepancies
V.   Targeting areas of concern
VI.   Devising plans to address concerns
VII. Implementing plans
VIII. Monitoring and evaluating progress
IX.   Revising plans if necessary
X.   Evaluating outcome

FIGURE 5.1. Enhancing Intimacy Program Overview

the couple is given a handout which outlines the entire program. This outline appears in Figure 5.1.

In order to illustrate the various aspects of the Enhancing Intimacy Program, a case example is presented in detail.

☐ Case Example: Clara and Ralph

Clara and Ralph had been formally engaged for six months when Clara contacted the author for premarital counseling. In the initial telephone conversation, she explained that ever since Ralph had given her an engagement ring he seemed to have become more distant and withdrawn. She said that prior to their engagement, she had felt very "close" to Ralph, but that lately she had been experiencing a "gulf" between them. She said that Ralph agreed that something had "changed" in their relationship and that some counseling might be helpful.

Clara and Ralph were seen together for their first interview the following week. Highlights of this interview are presented below:

Dr. B.: Good afternoon, Ralph.

Ralph: Good afternoon, Dr. B.

Dr. B.: Good afternoon, Clara.

Clara: Good afternoon, Dr. B. It is nice to meet you in person. Joan, who referred us to you, said you had been very helpful to her and Mike. I hope you can help us.

Dr. B.: Well, that was very nice of Joan to say that. She and Mike worked very hard to improve their relationship. I only facilitated their work together. I'll do what I can to help you both learn how to work together.

Clara: Thank you. I know that it really is up to us to work this through, but we need a little help from you.

Dr. B.: Fine. Have a seat on the sofa and tell me what you see as the difficulty. Who would like to start?

Clara: Well, I talked to you a little bit about what I think is the problem when I called you last week. Maybe Ralph should start today. (Clara turns toward Ralph.)

Ralph: Well, ever since Clara moved here from Florida to live with me, there has been tension in our relationship. Prior to that, we got along fine. You know, we had a long-distance relationship for about nine months. We saw each other every other weekend or so, and when it got serious Clara and I decided to live together.

Dr. B.: How was that decision made?

Clara: Well, it seemed like a natural progression. I was interviewing for jobs here in Atlanta. That was how we met. When I finally landed a job here, Ralph and I had already been dating for awhile. It was a logical step. You know, why move here and live alone when I would be spending most of my time with Ralph? Why pay two rents?

Ralph: Yes, we were getting pretty serious anyway. Clara moving in with me made sense.

Dr. B.: How did you feel about Clara moving in? I know it made logical sense, but sometimes logic and feelings are different.

Ralph: No, I felt very good about it. I didn't have any reservations.

Dr. B.: Clara, what about you? How did you feel?

Clara: I was very excited. I was tired of the long-distance deal. I really wanted to spend more quality time with Ralph.

Dr. B.: What were the circumstances leading up to your engagement? How was that decision made?

Clara: We had talked about getting engaged when I still lived in Florida. We picked out a ring shortly after I moved up here.

Dr. B.: Ralph, when did you first notice that there was a problem in your relationship with Clara?

Ralph: Well, I'm not certain.

Dr. B.: Anything stand out in your mind?

Ralph: (Sits silently for awhile.) Well, one thing.

Dr. B.: What was that?

Ralph: Well, it was during the "play-offs," you know, the NBA.

Clara: Well, it's not just the "play-offs." It's the Braves, it's the Falcons, it's the Bulldogs!

Ralph: Yeah, I guess I do watch a lot of sports. But that's how I relax. My job is stressful. Sports help me relax. I don't have to think. I just have to watch, but Clara says I shut her out. Maybe I do, but I don't mean to.

In this brief exchange, we begin to get some idea about the possible reasons for Ralph and Clara's intimacy problems. As often happens in long-distance relationships, couples do not have the opportunity to negotiate issues of closeness and separateness and interpersonal distance regulation until they begin to spend more time together.

Prospective spouses who do not live considerable distances from each other, who see each other on a daily basis or who live together, quickly begin to appreciate differences in their needs for intimacy. Although one might expect prospective mates to give serious consideration to major differences in intimacy needs before deciding to marry, this may not occur for a variety of reasons. These can be discovered by conducting a detailed intimate relationships history, as outlined earlier in Chapter 2. A summary of both Clara's and Ralph's intimate relationships histories illustrates this point.

Clara

Clara was the youngest of four children, all girls. Clara was her parents' (predominantly her father's) last attempt to have a son. Her father could not conceal his disappointment when he learned that another daughter had been born. When Clara was born, her oldest sister, Dora, was eleven. The second oldest child, Cynthia, was nine. Rhonda, her third sister, was six. By the time Clara was eleven, both Dora and Cynthia no longer lived with the family, and Rhonda was about to leave home to attend college.

Clara's father was a career military officer who spent much of his time away from his family. She was always the "little sister" who grew up in a "matriarchal environment." She was very close to her mother and Rhonda. When Rhonda finally left home, Clara felt an extreme sense of loss. She described what appears to have been a period of depression following Rhonda's departure. Her only consolation came from three classmates, girls she had befriended in first grade. This "foursome," as she referred to their relationship, was inseparable. It replicated her family life with her sisters—with only one difference—they all were the same age; they were peers, she no longer was the "little sister." This cohesive relationship continued throughout college. Even though the four women attended different universities, they came together for holidays and summer vacations. However, as each of the women married and moved to different parts of the United States, they were unable to meet frequently as a group. Nevertheless, they kept in frequent touch by phone and e-mail.

Clara was the last of the "foursome" to marry. She had not dated much during college. Most of her time had been spent studying and playing varsity tennis. Her excellent grades and athletic ability were two things of which her father took notice, and for which he gave her considerable praise and recognition. This was their only common ground. She had struggled throughout her life to win her father's love—to be validated by him. Achieving in a man's world was what he respected. She, therefore, chose a career in which few women excelled. The more success she gained, the more interest he showed. This both pleased and infuriated Clara. She began to realize that she had not been living her life for herself, but rather to win her father's approval. This need for approval from men even tainted the relationships she had with her lovers. She could not be truly intimate (except sexually) with men, she discovered, because she feared they might consider her intimacy needs to be a sign of weakness. She thus decided to live her life for herself. She began to explore new career options—ones that would be more self-fulfilling. This quest for personal fulfillment brought her to Atlanta, where she met Ralph.

Ralph

Ralph was an only child whose parents divorced when he was 9 years old. After his parents' divorce, Ralph and his mother moved in with his maternal grandparents. At an early age, Ralph felt responsible for taking care of his mother, both emotionally and financially. He got his first after-school job when he was 12. He gave his mother a percentage of his earnings, even though she protested, and saved the rest for his college education. Throughout high school, while other boys his age were "out having fun," Ralph was studying and working. There was "no time for girls," and he certainly did not choose to spend his money "going out on dates." Ralph did not develop a close group of friends his own age. He felt more at home with adults. Adults also seemed to like Ralph. They respected his work ethic and his commitment to his studies. He "is a serious young man" one of his mother's friends remarked when Ralph was only 14 years old.

In college, Ralph dated casually. He was very respectful of women, and enjoyed their company. He knew, however, that he could not become seriously involved with a woman until he was financially secure. After graduation, Ralph was employed by a computer software company. He advanced rapidly and became a team leader in a relatively short period of time. A promotion within the company required that he relocate to Atlanta. Several bonuses for outstanding performance in his new position enabled Ralph to afford a substantial down payment on a town house. With his career on track and his low monthly mortgage payments, Ralph now had the security he needed and he could begin to consider having a serious relationship with a woman.

Shortly after purchasing his town house, Ralph met Gloria. Ralph described Gloria as being very unlike himself. She was a "free spirit" who really knew how to enjoy herself. She worked for an Atlanta-based airline. One of the perks of this job allowed her to fly almost anywhere in the world for virtually no cost. She and Ralph traveled together whenever possible. At first this was exciting for Ralph, but, as time went by, Ralph began to realize that Gloria was not ready to settle down. He began to wonder if she ever would be ready. During a trip to Germany, Ralph broached the topic of marriage and children. On some preconscious level, Ralph knew what Gloria's response would be even before she answered. She said that she loved him, that if she were to marry and have children he would be the one she would choose, but that was something she did not see herself doing in the near future. Shortly after this discussion took place, Ralph and Gloria's relationship cooled. They parted friends.

Ralph had two rather brief, unsuccessful relationships following his break up with Gloria. In both cases the women were kind and attentive, but neither was Ralph's "intellectual equal." Then Ralph met Clara.

Courtship

Joan, a member of the "foursome," introduced Clara to Ralph while Clara was visiting Joan and her husband during the Thanksgiving holiday. Ralph and Joan's husband, Mike, were friends who had met at their local health club. Ralph and Clara played doubles tennis with Joan and Mike on the Friday after Thanksgiving, then attended a college football game on the following Saturday. After brunch on Sunday morning at a neighborhood sports bar, Clara and Ralph spent a leisurely afternoon with Joan and Mike watching professional football on television.

When asked what attracted her to Ralph, Clara said that he was "kind, considerate, and respectful." She said that he behaved like a "southern gentleman." She described him as being "reserved," but having an "understated power." Most of all, however, Ralph seemed to take a genuine interest in her "as a person." He did not "come on" to her nor try to "impress" her like other men she had known. Being with Ralph was "easy." There was "no pressure." Therefore, Clara was surprised and pleased when Ralph expressed an interest in seeing her again on her next visit to Atlanta.

Ralph's description of his first meeting with Clara during the Thanksgiving holiday did not differ from hers in any detail. When Ralph was asked to discuss his initial attraction to Clara, he focused upon her "sensibleness." He described her as "intelligent" and "down-to-earth." Of course, he found her to be "attractive" and "athletic," two qualities he liked in a woman, but the overriding attraction was her sense of being "grounded," of knowing where she was going and what she wanted from life. He admired the fact that she had the "guts" and "self-confidence" to explore new career paths instead of staying with a sure thing, where she had been very successful. In Clara, Ralph saw all the qualities he desired in a wife. He thought that if he did not pursue her he would regret it for the rest of his life, so pursue her he did.

Some Dynamics of Mate Selection and Relationship Development

In an earlier volume, Bagarozzi and Anderson (1989) described a process of mate selection wherein individuals actively seek out and attempt to marry persons whom they believe will act in accordance with an internal cognitive ideal model of one's spouse-to-be. This ideal does not connote perfection but represents a comparative standard by which potential spouses are measured, evaluated, compared, and judged. This cognitive matching process is both conscious and unconscious. Research has shown (Lewis & Spanier, 1979) that in the initial stages of relationship formation, physical attraction is important, and similarity on a number of salient dimensions plays a large part in whether the relationship will move forward toward greater levels of self-disclosure and intimacy (e.g., race, ethnic background, religion, socioeconomic status, intelligence, age, and value similarity).

As the relationship develops, however, more subtle and less tangible factors become more important in determining whether the relationship will continue or dissolve. These factors include the fulfillment of complementary needs (intimacy being one of these needs), a satisfactory role fit between the persons as these relate to husband/wife role expectations, and the spouses' actual role performances. The greater the congruence between an individual's expectations and the actual behavioral performances of his or her spouse, the higher the quality of the marriage.

Experiences with significant members of the opposite sex and repeated exposure to familial models and other male/female relationships (as mentioned earlier) contribute to the development of conscious and unconscious cognitive representations of one's ideal spouse and one's ideal marriage.

When the behavior of one's prospective spouse is perceived to fit and be in accordance with one's ideal, cognitive matching and congruency are said to have taken place. However, when the behavior of one's prospective spouse is perceived as deviating too drastically from one's ideal, a cognitive disequilibrium results, leading to intrapersonal stress, anxiety, frustration, etc. At such times, a person will behave in ways designed to restore congruence between his or her spouse-to-be and his or her ideal.

A variety of strategies, both cognitive and behavioral, can be employed to deal with such discrepancies:

1. The first option available to someone who consciously perceives a gross mismatch between his or her ideal and a perceived spouse-to-be is to end the relationship with the unsuitable candidate and to begin another search for a different candidate who more closely approximates the ideal.
2. The next option is for the cognitive ideal to undergo some modification by assimilation and accommodation to external realities. When this occurs, discrepancies are reduced and the ideal becomes more closely aligned with the perceived spouse-to-be.
3. The third option is more problematic, because it requires the use of unconscious defense mechanisms to distort what are clearly gross ideal/perceived discrepancies (e.g., denial, rationalization, intellectualization, repression).
4. The fourth option that can be used to deal with ideal/perceived discrepancies is for the person to attempt to bring about actual changes in his or her prospective spouse so that the spouse is molded into becoming a tintype of the ideal. Attempts to change one's spouse-to-be can be subtle or they can be blatant. They can be attempted during the courtship period or after the marriage has taken place.

In his clinical work over the years, the author has found that the more couples use options three and four to deal with ideal/perceived discrepancies over time, the more seriously distressed the relationship/marriage will tend to become. In some cases, however, a more pernicious and insidious process takes place during courtship, namely, the deliberate misrepresentation of the self to one's partner or spouse-to-be. Individuals who perpetrate such behavior have an uncanny ability to know how to act in a manner that mimics or simulates the unsuspecting partner's ideal. Such deceptive behavior is usually symptomatic of severe pathology.

The importance of taking a thorough history of each partner's intimate relationships cannot be stressed enough, because it is through these histories that one can gain access to each partner's ideal. Once ideal/perceived discrepancies have been identified, the therapist can begin to explore how each partner chose to deal with these discrepancies. For both Clara and Ralph, these ideal/perceived discrepancies did not become apparent until they began to live together. Essentially, Clara and Ralph were struggling with option #2—modifying their preexisting ideals—when they came in for premarital counseling. From Ralph's perspective, he was trying to reconcile his initial impressions and experiences with Clara, which were very congruent with his ideal, to his later, somewhat different impressions.

Initially, Ralph had seen an independent, attractive, athletic woman who was serious, levelheaded, and self-sufficient; a woman with whom he shared similar values and goals for their relationship and for their future. He had always wanted to marry someone who was self-sufficient, someone he would not feel responsible for taking care of emotionally and financially—like he had felt about his relationship with his mother. As their relationship progressed, however, Clara's needs for psychological and emotional intimacy were seen by him as "needy" and "dependent." This frightened Ralph, and he began to withdraw.

Clara, on the other hand, was baffled by Ralph's withdrawal. She thought that she had finally met a man who validated and appreciated her for who she really was, a man she could open up to and confide in, a man with whom she could become vulnerable and not be perceived as being weak. Unfortunately, the more she talked about her feelings and her fears, the more Ralph seemed to shut her out.

In Chapter 4, the importance of functional communication as a foundation skill for successful marriages was stressed. A critical component of the Enhancing Intimacy Program, therefore, is communications training. In Chapter 2, a number of dysfunctional communication practices were outlined (e.g., lying, hidden messages, mixed messages, paradoxical communications, aggressive communications) as were receiver dysfunctions (e.g., poor attending, defensiveness). The communications training model developed for use in this program was designed to eliminate dysfunctional sender and dysfunctional receiver practices. It places great emphasis upon helping couples develop skills in empathic listening and empathic responding. As spouses become more empathic and less egocentric, they begin to have a better understanding of each other. As a result of this increased understanding, ideal/perceived discrepancies become reduced through the complementary processes of assimilation and accommodation that facilitate changes in cognitive ideals.

The extent to which couples require training in the development of these empathic communication skills varies greatly. Some couples may be able to master these skills after only one or two training sessions. Others, however, may require as many as four to six closely supervised training sessions. The inability to acquire these skills or the reluctance to use these skills once they have been acquired should serve as a red flag to therapists. In many cases, an inability to learn empathic communication skills may be symptomatic of a serious psychological disturbance or personality disorder. A reluctance to use these skills once they have been successfully learned, however, should be taken as a sign that the individual (or the couple, if both partners are unwilling) does not wish to improve the relationship. In such cases, the therapist must question whether the relationship is more distressed than it appears or than test scores show (e.g., SIDCARB).

☐ Assessment of the Couple's Relationship Skills and Interpersonal Competencies

In order to evaluate this couple's communication skills, joint problem-solving strategies, decision-making capacities, and goal-setting capabilities, Clara and Ralph were assigned a behavioral task. The following instructions were given to them:

Assignment # 1

"Identify an area in your lives where there is a problem that is confronting you as a couple. This problem should *not* represent a conflict between you, but one that affects your relationship and which you must work on together, as a team, to solve. Once you have agreed upon the problem, develop a plan to resolve the problem, and decide what role each of you will play to make sure that the problem gets resolved."

A rating sheet is used to evaluate couples' skills in communication. Each partner is rated on a 10-point Likert scale. A sample sheet for rating communication effectiveness is presented in Figures 5.2 and 5.3.

Sender Skills	Never				Sometimes				Always	
1. Speaks directly to partner	1	2	3	4	5	6	7	8	9	10
2. Looks at partner when speaking	1	2	3	4	5	6	7	8	9	10
3. Speaks for self, uses "I" statements	1	2	3	4	5	6	7	8	9	10
4. Makes distinction between thoughts and feelings	1	2	3	4	5	6	7	8	9	10
5. Uses aggressive communications:	1	2	3	4	5	6	7	8	9	10
(a) attacks	1	2	3	4	5	6	7	8	9	10
(b) threatens	1	2	3	4	5	6	7	8	9	10
(c) blames	1	2	3	4	5	6	7	8	9	10
(d) criticizes	1	2	3	4	5	6	7	8	9	10
(e) ridicules	1	2	3	4	5	6	7	8	9	10
6. Lies to partner	1	2	3	4	5	6	7	8	9	10
7. Sends hidden or coded messages	1	2	3	4	5	6	7	8	9	10
8. Qualifies messages nonverbally	1	2	3	4	5	6	7	8	9	10
9. Qualifies messages verbally	1	2	3	4	5	6	7	8	9	10
10. Uses sarcasm	1	2	3	4	5	6	7	8	9	10
11. Sends confused or mixed messages	1	2	3	4	5	6	7	8	9	10
12. Sends paradoxical messages	1	2	3	4	5	6	7	8	9	10
13. Other	1	2	3	4	5	6	7	8	9	10

FIGURE 5.2. Communication.

Receiver Skills	Never				Sometime				Always	
1. Looks at speaker	1	2	3	4	5	6	7	8	9	10
2. Listens attentively, waits turn to speak	1	2	3	4	5	6	7	8	9	10
3. Lacks concentration, is distracted	1	2	3	4	5	6	7	8	9	10
4. Interrupts speaker	1	2	3	4	5	6	7	8	9	10
5. Becomes defensive:	1	2	3	4	5	6	7	8	9	10
(a) rebuttal	1	2	3	4	5	6	7	8	9	10
(b) counterattacks/counterargues	1	2	3	4	5	6	7	8	9	10
(c) cross complains	1	2	3	4	5	6	7	8	9	10
6. Attempts to read partner's mind	1	2	3	4	5	6	7	8	9	10
7. Misinterprets what partner says	1	2	3	4	5	6	7	8	9	10
8. Attributes malintention to partner's remarks	1	2	3	4	5	6	7	8	9	10
9. Finds hidden meaning in partner's remarks	1	2	3	4	5	6	7	8	9	10
10. Accepts partner's remarks at face value	1	2	3	4	5	6	7	8	9	10
11. Verbally disqualifies what partner says	1	2	3	4	5	6	7	8	9	10
12. Nonverbally disqualifies what partner says	1	2	3	4	5	6	7	8	9	10
13. Can restate or paraphrase what partner says	1	2	3	4	5	6	7	8	9	10
14. Other	1	2	3	4	5	6	7	8	9	10

FIGURE 5.3. Communication.

Guidelines for evaluating a couple's problem-solving, decision-making, goal-setting, and planning skills are presented in Figure 5.4.

In order to evaluate Clara and Ralph's ability to resolve interpersonal conflicts concerning issues of intimacy in their relationship, the couple was asked to complete the following assignment:

Assignment #2

"I would like you to take a few minutes to review, together, the Intimacy Needs Surveys you completed earlier. Once you have done this, select an intimacy issue that is a source of conflict in your relationship. Try as best you can to resolve this issue in a way that is satisfying for both of you and makes you feel good about yourselves and your relationship together."

Guidelines for evaluating a couple's success in negotiating and resolving conflicts over issues of intimacy are shown in Figure 5.5.

1. Can identify a problem in clear and behaviorally specific terms.		Yes	No
2. Can identify a variety of realistic solutions.		Yes	No
3. Can select one solution that is believed to be the best for problem solution/resolution.		Yes	No
4. Can develop concrete behavioral plans that can be implemented.		Yes	No
5. Can develop criteria for evaluating success.		Yes	No

FIGURE 5.4. Problem identification, decision making, goal setting and planning.

☐ Clara and Ralph: Review of Assessment Findings

Based upon Clara's and Ralph's responses to the SIDCARB, their relationship was perceived by both as being voluntary with medium levels of satisfaction (box #11 as depicted in Figure 4.3, page 53).

No sender or receiver difficulties of any consequence were observed in the couple's communication patterns as they worked their way through Assignment #1. However, communication problems did emerge, as did difficulties in conflict negotiation, as Clara and Ralph attempted to com-

1. Can identify an intimacy conflict in a clear and behaviorally specific manner.		Yes	No
2. Can identify his or her own contribution to the maintenance of the problem (e.g., behavioral, attitudinal, verbal, nonverbal).		Yes	No
3. Can identify partner's contribution to conflict maintenance without being accusatory, judgmental, blameful, etc.		Yes	No
4. Can accept partner's feedback without becoming defensive.		Yes	No
5. Is willing to negotiate change and make compromises in order to resolve conflict.		Yes	No
6. Is willing to change behaviors, attitudes, etc. in order to resolve conflict.		Yes	No

FIGURE 5.5. Conflict negotiation.

plete Assignment #2 (i.e., interpersonal conflict over issues of intimacy). During this assignment, Clara would become frustrated when she perceived Ralph as not being attentive and not listening to her. At these times, she would criticize Ralph for his "lack of empathy"; Ralph, in response, would "shut down" (i.e., not look at Clara while she was speaking, and nonverbally disqualify her comments). When this occurred, neither Ralph nor Clara was able to objectively discuss their respective contributions to and maintenance of the conflict. Neither could accept feedback from the other once the couple reached this point in the discussion.

Figure 5.6 shows Intimacy Needs Survey scores for Ralph and Clara. A review of this figure reveals that in all those component needs areas where Clara and Ralph reported Reciprocity and/or Receptivity dissatisfactions, the levels of dissatisfaction were not extreme. Satisfaction percentages for Clara in those areas she identified as problematic ranged from 60% to 67%; Ralph's satisfaction percentages in the three areas he identified as being of some concern were 67%. Therefore, one would not expect that helping Clara and Ralph achieve higher levels of intimacy satisfaction would pose too much of a problem—provided that both Clara and Ralph were willing to do what was needed to improve their relationship, namely, to learn the requisite skills and make the behavioral and attitudinal changes necessary to achieve greater intimacy in these areas.

☐ Feedback Session with Clara and Ralph

Presenting assessment findings to a couple is an extremely important aspect of the therapeutic process, because the manner in which assessment findings are interpreted to the couple will affect the couple's attitudes and motivation to complete the work necessary to improve their relationship. Part of the feedback session conducted with Ralph and Clara is reported below:

Dr. B.:   Good afternoon. Good to see you.

Clara: Thank you.

Ralph: Good to see you too, Dr. B.

Dr. B.:   Last time we completed the assessment phase of our work with a few assignments—the problem-solving and conflict negotiation tasks. I would like to begin today by reviewing with you all assessment results. Is that all right with you?

Clara: Yes.

Ralph: Fine.

Dr. B.:   Well, the first thing I would like to focus on is the SIDCARB find-

Section I	Section II	Section III	Section IV
Component Needs Strengths	Receptivity Satisfaction	Reciprocity Satisfaction	Time Satisfaction

	Ralph	Clara		Ralph	Clara		Ralph	Clara	Satisfaction Now
I Emotional	54	90		88%	67%		100%	67%	R Yes X No ___
II Psychological	56	81		88%	67%		100%	67%	C Yes ___ No X
III Intellectual	64	56		88%	88%		100%	100%	Minimum Time
IV Sexual	64	72		67%	67%		67%	100%	Hours Minutes
V Spiritual	64	64		100%	100%		100%	100%	R 1 ___
VI Aesthetic	64	56		100%	100%		100%	100%	C 2 ___
VII Social/Recreational	64	72		67%	60%		100%	60%	Desired Time
VIII Physical	64	72		88%	100%		100%	67%	Hours Minutes
									R 1 ___
Total Needs Score	494	563							C 2 ___

Comments	Comments	Comments	Comments
Both Clara's and Ralph's Total Intimacy Needs scores fall within the average range.	Ralph dissatisfied in 2 areas: Sexual and Social/Recreational. Clara dissatisfied in 4 areas: Emotional, Psychological, Sexual, and Social/Recreational.	Ralph dissatisfied in 1 area: Sexual. Clara dissatisfied in 4 areas: Emotional, Psychological, Social/Recreational, and Physical	

FIGURE 5.6. Intimacy Needs Survey Summary sheet for Ralph and Clara.

73

ings. The SIDCARB is this brief instrument—the one that looks at overall satisfaction in 10 areas of your relationship. (Dr. B. shows SIDCARB forms to Clara and Ralph.)

Clara: O.K.

Ralph: Fine.

Dr. B.:   Overall, your scores show that you are fairly well satisfied with your relationship. You don't seem to want many changes in each other's behavior, you are committed to this relationship, and you both express a sincere willingness to do the work necessary to improve it.

Clara: Yes, I think we are both very committed. I don't want to speak for Ralph, but I feel we both are (turns and looks at Ralph).

Ralph: This is true. I really want to make things better.

Dr. B.:   Good. The only two areas where you both would like some changes are those areas which, not surprisingly, are directly related to the problem that brought you in to see me, that is, intimacy. The two areas you identified are "communication" and "expressions of love and affection."

Clara: That makes sense to me. Sometimes we communicate very well, but other times it's not so good.

Ralph: I agree. I have no problem with all those other areas. It really is the communication and the intimacy that is the problem.

Dr. B.:   Well, actually, you communicate pretty well overall. You did very well on the problem-solving assignment, but you had a hard time with the interpersonal conflict negotiation task—the one which asked you to select an intimacy issue that was a source of conflict for you.

Clara: Yes, I know I gave Ralph a hard time with that one.

Dr. B.:   Ralph, what do you think about Clara's statement? Do you think she was giving you a hard time?

Ralph: Absolutely! She starts to accuse me, and it isn't very pleasant.

Dr. B.:   How does it make you feel when Clara accuses you?

Ralph: I want to get away from her.

Dr. B.:   You'd like to get away. I understand, but what do you feel? What do you experience?

Ralph: I get mad and I feel boxed in.

Dr. B.:   Is that when you begin to shut down?

Ralph: Yes.

Dr. B.:   You can't get away physically so you get away emotionally.

Ralph: I guess you might say that.

Dr. B.:   Clara, any thoughts?

Clara: When he gets like that, he's miles away.

Dr. B.:   And you're left out, Clara.

Clara: Yes.

Dr. B.:   Well, I think I can teach you how to resolve such conflicts in a way that will bring you closer together instead of putting distance between you.

Clara: I hope so.

Ralph: That would be a change for the better.

Dr. B.:   Now, let's turn to the Intimacy Needs Survey results. These need a little more time to interpret. (Dr. B. gives Ralph and Clara each a copy of the scoring sheet.)

Dr. B.:   (Pointing to Section I) In this first section, each component need strength is shown for both of you. Eight component needs strengths are dealt with in the first three sections. Time, the ninth component, is dealt with in the fourth section. For sections one, two, and three, Ralph, your scores are entered in the left-hand column. Clara, yours appear in the right-hand column.

Ralph: O.K.

Clara: I understand.

Dr. B.:   For each of you, your Total Needs Strength scores appear at the bottom, where it says "Total Needs Score." On average, scores range from 450 to 600. You can see that both of your scores fall well within the average range. Ralph, yours is 494. Clara, yours is 563.

Clara: Well, it is good to know we are both normal.

Dr. B.:   You seem surprised.

Clara: Yes. I guess I always thought that I had a very high need for intimacy, and I guess I was starting to think that Ralph's was pretty low.

Dr. B.:   Well, if you had discovered that you and Ralph actually did have a large need discrepancy, what would that have meant to you?

Clara: Well, if my needs were too high, I might be abnormal and Ralph, or anybody for that matter, would not be able to satisfy them, and I'd be very unhappy all my life. This is a very good sign.

Dr. B.:   Ralph, what are your thoughts and feelings about your Total Needs score and how it compares with Clara's?

Ralph: I feel good about them, but I notice that our needs for Emotional and Psychological intimacy are pretty different.

Dr. B.:   This is true, they are different, but they may not be a serious problem.

Ralph: What do you mean?

Clara: Yes, explain that.

Dr. B.:   Well, needs strengths differences are not as important as one's perceived satisfaction. For example, Clara, your need for Emotional intimacy is 90. Ralph, yours is 54. However, Ralph, for both Receptivity and Reciprocity satisfactions, you are able to meet Clara's needs at the 67% level. Similarly, Clara's need for Psychological intimacy is 81, and Ralph, yours is 56. Again, in both Reciprocity and Receptivity satisfaction, you are able to satisfy Clara's needs for Psychological intimacy at a 67% level.

Ralph: Yes, I see what you're talking about. It doesn't seem that bad when you look at it this way. I almost got a passing grade (laughs).

Dr. B.:   (Smiling) I think Clara will have to determine what a passing grade is for her, and you will be the judge of what is a passing grade for you when we look at those areas of intimacy where you are not 100% satisfied.

Clara: It is not the actual numbers then, it's the satisfaction the person experiences.

Dr. B.:   Right. Satisfaction is subjective. Highly subjective. That's why it is so important to be able to communicate your needs and wants clearly. We should not expect our partners to know what we need and what we want automatically. We have to ask for what we need and desire.

Clara: I know that intellectually, but sometimes, I don't want to have to ask Ralph.

Dr. B.:   I guess we are all guilty of that from time to time.

Clara: I guess.

Ralph: Me too. Sometimes I want Clara to know what I want, without saying so.

Dr. B.:   The communication training we will be doing later in the session will help both of you to be more direct with each other. Not only will that help both of you get what you want from each other more successfully, it will also bring you closer together. It will increase intimacy.

Clara: Even though our needs may be different?

Dr. B.:   I don't think people's intimacy needs change very much. I haven't seen any research that shows that they do, but that doesn't mean you can't learn how to satisfy each other's needs more successfully. For example, just being able to listen well, being empathic with one's partner, being non-judgmental—all these skills will increase feelings of intimacy. You know, Receptivity satisfaction. The need doesn't change, but when a person feels understood, when a person feels heard, intimacy increases.

Ralph: I never thought of it in those terms.

Dr. B.:   The same is true for Reciprocity satisfaction. Just using a few simple communication skills can increase satisfaction.

Clara: It sounds so simple.

Dr. B.:   Learning the skills is simple. The hard part is putting into practice, outside this office, what you have learned. That's the reason, as you know, for the homework assignments.

Clara: (Nods)

Dr. B.:   Let's return to the Intimacy Needs Survey Summary sheet.

Ralph: O.K.

Clara: O.K.

Dr. B.:   The other areas where satisfaction falls below the 70% level are Sexual intimacy, Social/Recreational intimacy, and Physical intimacy. Here again, satisfaction percentages are not that low.

Feedback as an Induction Process

The feedback session is much more than an information sharing process that takes place between the therapist and the couple. It can be conceptualized as an induction process where hope for a successful outcome is engendered by the therapist. The first thing that the reader will notice is that all assessment findings are presented in a positive light to the couple. For example, when SIDCARB findings are shared with the couple, rather than focusing on "medium levels of satisfaction," the therapist uses the phrase "fairly well satisfied" and then follows up with three additional positives, namely, the couple does not want many changes, the couple is committed to the relationship, and the couple expresses a sincere willingness to do the work necessary to improve their relationship. The effect of this positive approach can be seen in both Clara's and Ralph's responses.

Next, the therapist ties in SIDCARB findings with the couple's presenting problem. This is done to demonstrate the close relationship among communication, expressions of love and affection, and intimacy, thereby underscoring the importance of communication skills training which is an essential component of the program. When Clara and Ralph begin to focus on the negative aspects of their communication practices, the therapist switches the focus to what they do well. He does not deny that there are some communication difficulties, but he talks about these difficulties in a way which encourages the couple. He points to the fact that it is only one aspect of their communication that is problematic. He then characterizes their problem as a skills deficit, something over which they have control and something they can learn to correct. Mastering these skills will ultimately bring them closer together. The theme of functional communication being a skill that can be mastered permeates the feedback process. Similarly, Dr. B. presented Intimacy Needs Survey findings to Clara and Ralph, he did so in a way that normalized their differences by describing their Total Needs Strengths scores as falling within the "average range." He then talked about Receptivity and Reciprocity *satisfaction levels,* as opposed to *dissatisfaction levels,* thus emphasizing the positive aspects of their relationship.

There is a subtle cognitive intervention that takes place throughout the feedback process. The therapist says that the changes the partners will have to make in order to achieve greater intimacy and relationship satisfaction are minor and behavioral. Frequently, individuals entering counseling or psychotherapy are afraid that they will be required to make major changes in themselves, their personalities, and so forth. Such beliefs often trigger the mobilization of defensive resistance. However, when the therapist indicates that only small behavioral changes are necessary to bring about considerable improvement, defensiveness is reduced, since the integrity of the person is not threatened. Finally, the therapist emphasizes the importance of completing homework assignments and the need for practice. Again, the skills learning dimension is reinforced. More subtle, however, is the therapist's message that the power to improve the relationship rests with the couple.

Returning to Figure 5.6, we see that both Receptivity and Reciprocity satisfactions fall below the 70% levels for Ralph in the area of Sexual intimacy. Clara, on the other hand, reports a 67% satisfaction level only for Receptivity in this area. She also reports a 67% level of Receptivity satisfaction for Physical intimacy. Finally, both Ralph and Clara identify Social/Recreational intimacy as a source of concern. The way the therapist handles these findings with the couple is shown below:

Dr. B.:   I notice that you both have identified Social and Recreational intimacy as a problem for you.

Clara: Yes, Ralph spends too much time watching sports on TV and going to sports events with his friends.

Ralph: I know that's a sore spot for you, Clara, but you knew I was a sports nut when you met me, and I thought you shared my interests, you being a tennis player and all that.

Clara: True, I do like sports, but there is a limit. There are other things we can do aside from sports.

Ralph: I know (becomes silent).

Dr. B.:   I suspect that your earlier impressions of each other in this area may need to undergo some revision. You know, as we get to know each other better, first impressions may not hold up very well. I have found this to be true in all relationships. However, in long-distance relationships, sometimes it is more pronounced.

Ralph: Well, it is not only in the area of sports and recreation. There is also a problem in our sex life.

Dr. B.:   Yes, I noticed that you flagged that area while Clara, (turns to Clara) you seem to be more satisfied with this aspect of intimacy than Ralph is. I wonder if this might be another one of those areas where initial impressions or initial experiences may not have been 100% reliable.

Clara: No, Dr. B. That's not so. I think I am the same sexual person I was when Ralph and I met, but Ralph has become less attentive since I moved up here. He still wants sex, but some of the tenderness, the caring, and the nonsexual physical stuff—you know, kissing and hand holding—has stopped.

Dr. B.:   Yes, Clara, I see that you identified Reciprocity satisfaction as falling below 70% for Sexual and Physical intimacy.

Clara: Yes. Sometimes I'd like Ralph to be physical without it always ending up sexual.

Dr. B.:   Ralph, what are your thoughts?

Ralph: Clara has said that before. I've heard that before. I guess I am not as romantic as I was when she lived so far away and I missed her so much.

Reducing Perceived/Ideal Discrepancies

In this excerpt, the therapist begins to set the stage for the next step in the process of enhancing intimacy between Clara and Ralph—helping them develop more accurate perceptions of each other, namely, helping them reduce ideal/perceived discrepancies. Typically, this process begins during the communications training phase of the program and continues throughout its duration. Once partners have acquired functional communication skills, they are asked to use these new skills to discuss their initial impressions and perceptions of each other. Then, they are asked to compare and to contrast these initial impressions and perceptions with what they now believe to be more true and accurate descriptions of their partners. Since genuine intimacy can only be achieved through accurate knowledge and understanding of one's partner, reducing distortions as much as possible is seen as being extremely important. Developing functional communication skills is a crucial component of the couple's efforts to reduce distortion in their perception of one another.

Functional communication has been found to be associated with marital satisfaction in a number of research studies and is believed to be the foundation for a successful relationship. Contrary to popular belief, functional communication does *not* mean saying whatever you think or feel without regard for your partner's feelings. A couple's communication is said to be functional when:

1. The message sent by one partner (the sender) is the same message that is heard by the other partner (the receiver).
2. The communication increases the couple's level of understanding and empathy.
3. The communication reduces defensiveness.
4. The communication leads to joint problem solving and successful conflict resolution.
5. The communication leads to greater intimacy.

Guidelines for developing functional communication skills are presented in Figures 5.7 and 5.8. The skills to be learned are broken down into *Sender* skills and *Receiver* skills. The reader will note that both sets of skills are designed to correct the sender and receiver problems identified in Chapter 2.

To illustrate how the therapist begins the process of reducing ideal/perceived discrepancies and rectifying distortions, the following excerpt is offered.

1. Speak directly to your partner and look directly at your partner while speaking. Speak for yourself, not for your partner.

2. Take full responsibility for what you feel and experience. Speak from the "I position." For example

Say:	Do not say:
• "I feel hurt when you don't look at me when we are talking."	• "You hurt me" or "You make me feel hurt."
• "I feel angry when you don't keep your word."	• "You make me angry."
• "I feel happy when you say you love me."	• "You make me feel guilty."
	• "You make me feel happy"

3. Do not confuse what you think about something with how you feel about something. Separate your thoughts from your feelings. For example:

Say:	Do not say:
• "I think you are sincere."	• "I feel you are sincere."
• "I feel sad that you don't trust me."	• "I think it is sad that you don't trust me."

4. Do not "mind read" or attribute hidden meanings to your partner's behaviors or statements. Explain to your partner how you perceive and interpret his or her behavior. Keep in mind that these are your perceptions and interpretations and that they may not be accurate. For example:

Say:	Do not say:
• "Yesterday, before you left for work, you made the bed and put the dishes in the dishwasher. My interpretation of your behavior was that you were sending me a message that I am not a good housekeeper. *Am I correct in my interpretation?*"	• "Yesterday, before you left for work, you made the bed and put the dishes in the dishwasher. I know you did that to tell me that I am not a good housekeeper."

5. Say exactly what you mean. Do not send any hidden messages or expect your partner to read your mind. *Be direct*, but be *polite and diplomatic.* For example:

Say:	Do not say:
• "I don't like it when you drive my car and bring it back with the gas tank almost empty. Would you please refill the tank when you use my car in the future?"	• "Did you pass a gas station on the way home from work today?"

Continued

FIGURE 5.7. Sender guidelines.

6. Do not use aggressive forms of communication. Aggressive communications are those communications that are designed to hurt your partner. These types of statements do not help you to communicate accurately your position, and only lead to defensiveness, counterattacks, or withdrawal. Some of the most common types of aggressive communications are:

   (a) attacking one's partner
   (b) threatening one's partner
   (c) blaming one's partner
   (d) criticizing one's partner
   (e) ridiculing one's partner
   (f) using sarcastic speech and tone
   (g) interrupting one's partner

7. When you are speaking, speak in short and concise sentences. Speak for only a brief period of time, and do not monopolize the conversation. When you are through speaking, let your partner know. Ask your partner to summarize what you have said so that you can judge whether he or she has heard you accurately. If your partner has repeated what you have said correctly, indicate that he or she has done so by acknowledging that the message you were trying to send was accurately received by him or her.

FIGURE 5.7. Sender guidelines.

1. Listen attentively whenever your partner is speaking to you. Look directly at your partner while he or she is talking.
2. Do not interrupt your partner when he or she is speaking.
3. Accept whatever your partner says "at face value." Do not attribute hidden meanings to what your partner says. Take everything that is said literally. Do not "mind read" or "interpret" what is said.
4. Try to put yourself in your partner's place. Try to see the world and try to see yourself from your partner's perspective. Try to understand how he or she feels, how he or she sees things, and how he or she experiences you.
5. Try to empathize with your partner, to feel what your partner is feeling and what it must be like to be your partner. Try not to project your thoughts, feelings, ideas, values, etc., onto your partner.
6. Do not pass judgments about your partner's feelings, thoughts, beliefs, or viewpoints, even if you do not agree with them. Try to respect your differences.
7. When your partner is finished speaking, repeat back to him or her (in summary form) what you have heard and understood. This will help your partner know whether he or she has been heard and understood accurately.
8. If, for any reason, you are unclear or have not understood what your partner said, ask your partner for clarification or ask him or her to repeat the message or statement.
9. If you think that your partner has incorrectly interpreted your statement of behavior, or if you believe that your partner has misunderstood or misinterpreted your intentions, you should clarify what you said and explain what your true intentions were when it is your turn to speak.

FIGURE 5.8. Receiver guidelines.

Dr. B.:   Well, folks, you seem to have had very little trouble learning the communication skills last time and you were able to find the time to practice them over the past week. Was there any difficulty with the homework assignment I gave you at the end of last week's session?

Clara: No. Actually, I found it to be very helpful for me. You asked us to practice our communication skills by talking about what we liked about each other and what we believed to be the positive aspects of our relationship, right?

Dr. B.:   Yes, that's correct.

Clara: Well, that assignment really helped me realize what a nice person Ralph really is (Clara turns to Ralph).

Ralph: Same here, Doc. It helped me appreciate Clara more. I didn't realize that I had been neglecting her, and it really paid off (Ralph laughs).

Dr. B.:   In what way did it pay off?

Ralph: We had some real good sex for the first time in a while.

Clara: (Blushing) Yes, I must admit it was very nice.

Dr. B.:   I am certainly happy for you. Sometimes couples have trouble with the first assignment, but that doesn't seem to have been an issue with you.

Clara: No. I think it was good. It turned out good in a number of respects.

Ralph: Yes, it was pretty good.

Dr. B.:   O.K. I'd like to have you focus on another issue, now. This next exercise has to do with helping you learn more about each other. It is designed to help you clear up some misconceptions you both might have.

Clara: Yes, O.K. That sounds good.

Ralph: O.K. Let's go.

Dr. B.: (The therapist then hands Clara and Ralph a copy of the Intimacy Needs Survey score sheet [Figure 5.6] and begins.) I'd like to return to this score sheet, and I'd like to begin by focusing on an area of intimacy that seems to be a source of tension and misunderstanding between you—Social and Recreational intimacy. I selected this area because I believe it to be one where you both have some inaccurate perceptions and some unverbalized expectations of each other.

What I would like you to do is to discuss, using the communication skills you learned so well, how you perceived each other's needs for Social and Recreational intimacy when you met, and compare those first impressions with what you now believe to be true about each other. Do you understand what I'd like you to do?

Clara: Yes.

Ralph: Yes, I do.

Dr. B.:   O.K. Who would like to begin?

Ralph: I'd like to start.

Dr. B.:   O.K. Ralph. Please speak directly to Clara. Clara, we'll start off with Ralph being the sender and you the receiver.

Clara: O.K.

Ralph: Well, Clara, when we first met I thought you really enjoyed sporting events. You remember that Thanksgiving weekend when we met at Joan and Mike's house? We played tennis. We went to see the Georgia Bulldogs play on Saturday, and then we watched football on TV the next Sunday.

Clara: Yes, I do. I remember we played tennis and went to the football game and watched the Falcons lose the next day.

Ralph: I really thought that you liked sports. You played tennis in college and when you visited me on the weekends or when I visited you before we were engaged, we watched a lot of sports—you know, the NBA, the Hawks, and the Braves. I don't remember you telling me that you didn't like watching sports programs.

Clara: Yes, Ralph, this is true. I watched all those sports events, and I never told you that I thought it was too much, and I'm sorry if you got the wrong impression.

Ralph: Can you tell me why you waited until after we were engaged to say something about it?

Clara: When we lived apart, the time I spent with you meant more to me than what we did when we were together. I don't mean to imply that you didn't make your interest in sports clear to me from the start, but I thought that once we were together more, you know, once we lived together and got married, that I'd have more time with you. I like sports too, but not as much as you do. I don't want you to think that I was being deceitful or dishonest, but I did think things would be different once we lived together.

Ralph: You're saying that our time together was more important than what we did together. You knew that I had a strong interest in sports, and you didn't expect that to change, but you expected me to spend more time with you, not doing sports things, once we were together.

Clara: Yes.

Dr. B.:   Clara, can you tell Ralph how you see him now?

Clara: Yes (turns toward Ralph). I think you have more interest in sports than you have in our relationship, and I feel sad about that. I am afraid that, as time goes on, you will take less and less interest in me, and, when we have children, you will take even less interest in us.

Ralph: I'm not sure I understand. When you say I'll take less interest in "us," who do you mean?

Clara: I mean our children and me, and I don't know if that is something I can live with. No, that is something I won't live with.

Ralph: I see.

Clara: Ralph, I know this is a touchy issue, but I feel compelled to bring it up.

Ralph: O.K.

Clara: O.K. Well, it's Gloria. You told me that one of the reasons you and

Gloria broke it off was because she was not ready to marry you and have children. Am I right?

Ralph: Yes, that's true.

Clara: That's what makes me so confused. You say you want to get married. You say you want to have children, yet you show so little interest in me. Sometimes I think I'm just an object—something to be used by you for whatever you desire. You know, someone to go to sporting events with, to have fun, to have sex, and to have your children.

Ralph: So you think I'm using you for fun, sex, and for having kids.

Clara: Yes. Sometimes I do, not all the time, but sometimes.

Ralph: Boy, that is a very nasty characterization of me. I certainly don't see myself that way. You make me sound like a chauvanist, you know, a real stereotype.

Clara: I'm sorry Ralph, but that is how I see you at times.

Ralph: (After a few moments of silence) I don't know what to say. I just don't see myself like that.

Dr. B.:   Clara, I admire your honesty and directness. Ralph, I know this is probably hard to hear.

Ralph: It is, Dr. B., because I'm really not like that. I chose Clara because she is beautiful and intelligent. I would never think of treating her like an object.

Dr. B.:   I'm sure that's true, Ralph. I don't experience you as someone who would deliberately treat Clara, or any woman for that matter, as an object, but that is what Clara experiences with you, from time to time. Those are her perceptions, and we tend to respond to people as we perceive them.

Ralph: That may be so, but I don't like how I am being perceived.

Dr. B.:   I understand. I suspect you feel misunderstood.

Ralph: Yes. Misunderstood and very frustrated. (Turns to Clara) I am sorry, Clara, I didn't realize how I was behaving.

Clara: Ralph, this is a very sensitive issue for me.

Ralph: I know it is. (Clara is silent).

Dr. B.:   Ralph, are there any other first impressions of Clara that don't seem to hold up now?

Ralph: Well, there is one other.

Dr. B.:   Yes.

Ralph: (Turning to Clara) Your indecisiveness.

Clara: My indecisiveness? I don't consider myself to be indecisive.

Ralph: Well, not in general, but for some major decisions you have been. Take the job thing, for example.

Clara: Yes.

Ralph: You obsessed about which job to take.

Clara: Obsess is too strong a word.

Dr. B.:   Let's try to avoid labeling each other's behavior.

Ralph: O.K., Doc. (Turns to Clara) But you did have a hard time making that decision. I remember. We talked about that decision for days. We talked on the phone, and we talked about it when you came up here for your interviews with the companies.

Clara: Yes, we did a lot of talking, but you never gave me any input. You never stated an opinion.

Ralph: Clara, that was your decision to make.

Clara: I know it was my decision to make. I didn't want you to make the decision for me. All I wanted from you was some support. Some input.

Ralph: Clara, I did not want to influence you in any way. I wanted it to be totally your own decision.

Dr. B.:   Clara, how did you interpret Ralph's not stating his opinion?

Clara: That he didn't care.

Dr. B.:   Ralph, what are your thoughts?

Ralph: I certainly did care. Because I respect you, it would not be right to try to influence your decision. The job you select should be your decision. You had to take a job that would be best for you and for your career—one that would make you happy and one that would be fulfilling. I wanted you to do what was best for you. I did not want to influence you in any way. I know you did a lot of things, especially in your work, to please your father, and I didn't want to get in that type of relationship with you.

Clara: Oh, I never thought of that. I don't see you as a father figure. You are not at all like my father. I just wanted your opinion. That would have felt supportive.

Dr. B.:   Ralph, your respect for Clara was perceived by her as a lack of support. Clara, your seeking Ralph's opinion was not seen as a request for support, but as indecisiveness.

Ralph: It was more than that, Dr. B., I saw it as dependence. One of the most attractive things about Clara was her self-sufficiency, her independence. When she had so much trouble making that decision, I became uneasy.

Dr. B.:   You are very sensitive, Ralph, about dependency in women, so you chose an independent woman—Clara. However, it seems that any behavior that you consider to be dependent frightens you, I think.

Ralph: You mean like we talked about in our individual sessions—you know, women like my mother?

Dr. B.:   Perhaps.

Ralph: I guess that's when I withdraw.

Dr. B.:   (To Clara) And you feel isolated.

Clara: Yes, he gets so distant.

In the preceding example, the therapist begins to deal with helping Clara and Ralph reduce ideal/perceived discrepancies and distorted perceptions of each other that are preventing them from developing a more intimate relationship. His intention is to help Clara and Ralph achieve a more accurate understanding of each other. Accurate understanding, in this context, means several things. First, it means that each partner's self-definition is perceived as being validated by his or her mate. Second, it means that each partner feels understood by his or her mate. Finally, it means that each partner feels that his or her true motives and intentions are understood and recognized by his or her mate. The reader will notice that the therapist does not positively reframe behaviors, meanings, or intentions. Each partner is asked to explain his or her behavior and motives so that there is no room for doubting what was meant or intended. The goals here are accurate understanding, self-validation, and the development of a system of shared meanings.

Helping couples reduce ideal/perceived discrepancies, as shown above, is an intimacy-enhancing technique that couples rarely experience as threatening, because it does not require each partner to make major behavioral changes; therefore, it can also be used to help couples who are seriously distressed. It can also be used to break through the resistance of individuals who fear that their partner (or the therapist) is going to require that they make substantial modifications in themselves or their personality makeups.

6
CHAPTER

Enhancing Intimacy: Practices and Procedures with Clara and Ralph Continued

☐ Overview

- Clara and Ralph: Treatment continued
- General strategies for dealing with needs discrepancies:
  Focusing the treatment
  Creating a couple-based team approach
  Using collaboration, cooperation, and joint problem solving
  Reframing, transformation, and externalization of the couple's problem
  Using homework assignments
  Dealing with emotional reactivity
  Fostering emotional and psychological differentiation
  A five-step approach to cognitive restructuring

In the previous chapter, we saw how the process of enhancing intimacy begins with the therapist teaching a couple how to use some very basic communications skills and verbal tools to correct faulty interpretations and impressions and discuss their attributions of malintention, thereby facilitating the process of reducing ideal/perceived discrepancies. In this chapter, some suggestions for helping couples deal with needs strengths differences are offered, and techniques for helping couples address Receptivity and Reciprocity dissatisfactions are presented.

The first step in dealing with needs discrepancies and dissatisfactions is to consider their magnitude. The greater the difference in Total Needs Strengths scores between individuals, the more difficult the therapist's task. Similarly, the lower Receptivity and Reciprocity satisfaction percentage scores are, the more difficult the therapeutic task. The next step is helping the couple set realistic treatment goals given the magnitude of their discrepancies and dissatisfactions. Let us return to the session with Ralph and Clara.

Dr. B.:   Let's see if we can begin, today, to deal with bridging the distance gap between you.

Ralph: Fine.

Clara: Good.

Dr. B.:   (Returning to the Intimacy Needs Survey scoring sheet) Do you remember, earlier in the session, we talked about your Total Intimacy Needs Strengths scores?

Clara: Yes.

Ralph: Yes.

Dr. B.:   As I said earlier, both of your scores are in the average range. What I didn't say was that the differences between your scores are not of a substantial magnitude. Ralph, your score of 494 is not very different from Clara's 563. When I say not substantially different, I am speaking about clinical differences and not statistical differences.

Ralph: I understand.

Clara: I know.

Dr. B.:   I consider that to be a positive, especially when you consider that both of your Receptivity and Reciprocity satisfaction scores are fairly high in those areas where you would like to increase your intimacy.

Clara: Well, that is encouraging.

Ralph: Yes, it is.

Dr. B.:   Well, what I usually do at this juncture in the session is to help the couple set some goals for our work together. Is that something you would like to do now, or is there another issue you would like to focus on— something that you think is unfinished?

Clara: No, nothing else.

Ralph: No, let's go on.

Dr. B.:   I usually ask couples to begin with an intimacy dimension that both partners have identified as a concern, preferably one where the satisfaction percentage is fairly high.

Clara: For us, that would be in the Social and Recreational area.

Dr. B.:   Yes, that's right. How would you both feel about returning to that area?

Clara: O.K.

Ralph: Fine.

Dr. B.:   (Handing Ralph and Clara a copy of Assignment #1) Do you remember this assignment that I gave you to do during the assessment process?

Clara: Yes.

Ralph: Yes.

Dr. B.:   Good. What I would like you to do is to try to resolve, as much as you possibly can, the concerns you have in the area of Social and Recreational intimacy. Treat these concerns not as conflicts between you but as problems confronting you as a couple—problems that you must resolve as a team, like you did so well during the assessment process.

Ralph: That is certainly an interesting way of looking at things.

Dr. B.:   Yes. It is a different perspective. I think it allows for more flexibility. It is a way of looking at things that can transform certain types of personal conflicts—not all of them, however—into external problems that can be approached cooperatively and collaboratively. I believe that the more I can help couples learn to approach differences this way, the more satisfaction they will experience in their relationship.

Clara: That makes sense.

Dr. B.:   I think so, too. Now, what I'd like you to do is to identify one issue in this area at a time. Try to define the issue in such a way that will make a behavioral solution possible. By behavioral solution, I mean a solution that will specify what each of you will agree to do in order to bring about a solution that is acceptable to both of you. Are my directions clear?

Ralph: Yes.

Clara: Yes.

Dr. B.:   O.K. Who would like to start?

Ralph: I'd like to start.

Clara: O.K.

Dr. B.:   O.K. Clara, remember to summarize what Ralph says before you take your turn. Ralph, you do the same.

Clara: O.K.

Ralph: O.K. I think the first thing that would be helpful for us to look at is our expectations in this area.

Clara: I agree. I'd like us to talk about our expectations.

Ralph: Well, I like to watch the local teams when their games are televised. Then, I like to watch the play-offs and the championship games at the end of the seasons.

Clara: The televised games, the play-offs, and the championship games.

Ralph: Yes.

Clara: That seems like an awful lot of time to me. It really eats into the time we can have together. I feel like I have to get my time in with you between games.

Ralph: You think it is too much time.

Clara: Yes. We both work, and sometimes we don't get home until about seven or eight o'clock at night. When the games are on at night, we watch them during dinner. I clean up and you watch the game when we are through. By the time the game is over, it's time to go to bed, and we've had no time together.

Ralph: You're saying I watch too much sports.

Dr. B.:   It seems to me, Ralph, that Clara is saying something more than that. It sounds like she is saying that she doesn't feel that she has enough time with you.

Clara: (To Ralph) Dr. B. is right. It is not the games as much as the time, but there is also the fact that you don't help me clean up. You leave me in the kitchen, and you go into the living room to watch the game.

Ralph: So it's not the games as much as the time and the fact that I don't help you.

Clara: Yes, and this only adds to my feelings of being an object. Someone who cooks and cleans up.

Dr. B.:   Can you approach this as two problems to solve as a couple—sharing time together and doing household tasks?

Clara: I think that would be a good start.

Ralph: Yes, we can try.

Clara: (To Ralph) Can we try to come up with a way of spending more time together?

Ralph: What do you suggest?

Dr. B.:   Ralph, rather than ask Clara to come up with a solution, why don't you give some thought as to what you might do so that more time can be spent together?

Ralph: O.K.

Dr. B.:   Clara, I'd like you also to think of what you might do so that you and Ralph can have some more time together.

Clara: All right.

Ralph: I guess I could wait until a little later in the evening to watch the games.

Clara: I don't think I'd mind you watching the games or watching a sports show after dinner, if you helped me clean up and then spent some time with me.

Ralph: That sounds good to me. We can clean up together, talk a little, and then I can watch some television.

Dr. B.:   (Turning to Clara who is frowning) Clara, the look on your face tells me that this solution does not seem to sit well with you. You seem to be frowning. Is that an accurate interpretation of your nonverbal behavior?

Clara: Yes.

Dr. B.:   Clara, can you tell Ralph what you are frowning about?

Clara: (Turning to Ralph) I think you will rush through the clean up, talk to me for a few minutes, and then switch on the television. I'm afraid that nothing will change.

Dr. B.: (To Ralph and Clara) Let's focus on one issue at a time. Let's stay with the time issue.

Ralph: O.K.

Clara: Fine.

Dr. B.: It might be helpful for both of you to think about how much time together would be desirable.

Ralph: Maybe a half hour each night, after dinner and before watching television or doing something else.

Clara: Half an hour would be great, especially if you helped me clean up.

Dr. B.: You both agree that an extra half hour each night would be acceptable to both of you?

Clara: Yes, I think so, if I got help from Ralph.

Ralph: Dr. B., we still practice our communications two nights a week for about a half hour, would that count?

Dr. B.: (To Ralph) Ask Clara how she feels about that. It is something you both must agree upon.

Clara: I have no problem with that.

Dr. B.: Do you have a set time on specific days when you practice?

Ralph: Yes. Monday evenings after dinner and Saturday mornings after breakfast.

Clara: Most of the time. Sometimes we don't get around to the Monday night practices when Monday Night Football is on.

Dr. B.: In my experience, I have found that if you can agree upon regular times, when nothing else is competing for that time, you can build in that time together so it becomes routine.

Clara: I see.

Ralph: I understand.

Dr. B.: Our time is just about up, now. Can you continue to work on scheduling time together as your homework for this week?

Clara: Sure.

Ralph: Yes.

Dr. B.: O.K. Keep up the good work.

Ralph: O.K.

Clara: See you next week.

In the above example, the therapist encouraged Clara and Ralph to apply their already demonstrated proficiency in problem solving to achieve greater intimacy. By asking them to treat their shared concerns in the area of Social and Recreational intimacy as problems confronting them as a couple, the therapist helps Clara and Ralph reframe and transform an interpersonal conflict into an external problem that can be solved through collaboration and cooperation. The reader will recall that in Chapter 2, four critical developmental tasks of childhood, according to Sullivan, were identified. Two of these tasks, the ability to collaborate and the ability to cooperate, were demonstrated by Clara and Ralph during the assessment process. Therefore, the therapist was able to ask them to call upon these strengths to resolve the problem at hand. The more successful couples are in transforming potential interpersonal conflicts into external problems that can be solved jointly, the more satisfaction they will experience and the more intimate they will feel. However, not all couples are able to make this cognitive readjustment and not all interpersonal conflicts between partners lend themselves to such a cognitive reorientation. There are some interpersonal conflicts that require a different set of skills and strategies. More will be said about this later.

In the author's work with couples who desire to become more intimate, time spent together as a couple is often an important issue for them to consider. For some couples, it is simply a matter of helping them spend more time together. For others, however, the length of time spent together is less important than what transpires between the partners when they are together. It doesn't matter whether the issue is the amount of time or the significance of what the couple does during their time, most therapists will find that the time factor inevitably surfaces as an issue to be dealt with sooner or later. By making weekly homework assignments an integral part of the couple's work from the outset of therapy, additional time together is subtly built into the relationship. For some couples, the extra hour or two spent together each week practicing the various skills they have learned in therapy is enough to satisfy the need for more intimate time. For others, like Clara and Ralph, an additional hour or two may be insufficient. When this is the case, an intervention such as the one used in the latest example may be helpful.

When homework assignments are given at the end of a session, the therapist should begin the next session by asking the partners if they had been able to complete the previous week's assignment. If a couple was unable to follow through on a given assignment, the therapist should explore the reasons for the couple's inability to do so. Couples may not complete homework assignments for a variety of reasons, for example, the therapist's directives were not clearly communicated, external forces beyond the couple's control prohibited the partners from completing the assignment, or resistance. Resistance should be suspected when the couple repeatedly fails to complete homework assignments. When resistance is believed to be the reason for repeated failure to complete homework assignments, an educational skills learning approach may not be appropriate. When this occurs, the possible reasons for the couple's resistance should be explored so that a program or procedure that is more in keeping with the couple's needs can be recommended.

Let us now return to Clara and Ralph.

Dr. B.:   Good afternoon, Clara.

Clara: Good afternoon.

Dr. B.:   Good afternoon, Ralph.

Ralph: Good afternoon, Dr. B.

Dr. B.:   I would like to begin today's session by asking you if you were able to complete the homework assignment that was given to you last week?

Clara: Yes, we did.

Ralph: Yes.

Dr. B.:   What solution or solutions did you agree upon?

Ralph: We agreed to spend three nights a week, after dinner and cleanup, taking a walk together, weather permitting.

Clara: Yes, we both want to exercise more so that would be good. We usually walk for about thirty-five minutes. We can talk while we are walking and I'd have Ralph's attention.

Ralph: (To Dr. B.) We still will practice our communication skills on Saturday, but we changed the weeknight to Tuesday so it doesn't compete with Monday Night Football.

Dr. B.:   Are both of you satisfied with this solution?

Clara: I am.

Ralph: Yes. It seems fair to me.

Dr. B.:   Good. Did you get a chance to resolve the issue of after-dinner cleanup?

Clara: Yes. On those nights when we are going to take our walk, I'll clean up and Ralph can watch television or read the paper or something like that. On the nights that we don't walk, Ralph will help me clean up and we can talk together during that time.

Dr. B.:   Are both of you satisfied with this solution?

Clara: I am.

Ralph: I am too. We have also agreed that if there is a major sports event or game that I'd like to see, we can turn it on while we are cleaning up.

Clara: Yes, that's O.K. I enjoy watching some of those events also.

Dr. B.:   Do you consider these issues of time, watching sports, and cleanup to be successfully resolved now?

Clara: Yes.

Ralph: I think so.

Dr. B.:   Fine. (Returning to the Intimacy Needs Survey score sheet) You really have done well tackling the issues that surfaced in the Social and Recreational area. The areas that remain to be dealt with are Emotional,

Psychological, Sexual, and Physical intimacy. Which one would you like to focus on next?

Clara: I'd like to talk about Emotional and Psychological intimacy first.

Dr. B.:   Ralph, what are your thoughts and feelings about Clara's suggestion?

Ralph: That's O.K. with me, but I want to make sure that we deal with our sex life. Since we have been coming to see you, we have had sex more frequently, but I still want to talk about this issue. I think we have some matters to clear up.

Clara: Yes, I agree. I don't want to neglect our sex life.

Dr. B.:   Ralph, are you O.K. with dealing with Sexual intimacy a little later?

Ralph: Yes.

Dr. B.:   Before you begin to discuss these two areas of intimacy, you might find it helpful to review the definitions of Emotional and Psychological intimacy and to review your responses to the Intimacy Needs Survey. (Dr. B. hands the Intimacy Needs Surveys to Ralph and Clara.) Take a few minutes to refresh your memories.

Clara: (After reviewing her responses, Clara turns toward Ralph.) Ralph, in the area of Emotional intimacy, I think you have been very receptive to me in most areas, but there are some times when I feel shut out by you.

Ralph: You think I am receptive in most areas of emotional intimacy, but I sometimes shut down, you think.

Clara: Yes, I do.

Ralph: What are those areas? What times do I shut down, as far as you are concerned?

Clara: Well, I'm not really sure.

Dr. B.:   Clara, are you aware of particular feelings that you express that you think cause Ralph to shut down? Is it the intensity of your expression? Is it your delivery, or could it be the content?

Clara: I think it might be all of the above. Sometimes, I think it's what I say. Sometimes I think it's how I say it, but I am never sure what Ralph's reaction will be.

Dr. B.:   That sounds frustrating.

Clara: Yes, and confusing.

Dr. B.:   Ralph, you agreed earlier that there are times when you do shut down.

Ralph: Yes, I can do that, yes.

Dr. B.:   Are you aware of what you might be responding to at those times—when you may not be totally receptive to Clara's feelings?

Ralph: I'm not completely sure, but it is more like a feeling response rather than a deliberate decision to shut down.

Dr. B.:   What is the feeling you experience?

Ralph: It's like a tenseness.

Dr. B.:   Where do you feel the tenseness?

Ralph: My jaw, my neck, and my head.

Dr. B.:   So, these are the cues that signal a shutdown?

Ralph: I guess you can call it that.

Dr. B.:   Ralph, are you aware of what you say to yourself at those times?

Ralph: What do you mean?

Dr. B.:   Clara says or does something. You begin to feel tense. Your jaw tightens. Your neck tightens, and your head hurts.

Ralph: Yes.

Dr. B.:   Then what do you think?

Ralph: I think, "Oh, no, here it comes."

Dr. B.:   What do you think is going to happen?

Ralph: I'm not sure, but something unpleasant.

Dr. B.:   Let me see if I've gotten the sequence right.

Ralph: O.K.

Dr. B.:   Clara does or says something and you become tense, and you say to yourself, "Oh, no, here it comes."

Ralph: Right.

Dr. B.:   Then what do you do?

Ralph: I get quiet. I don't know what to say.

Clara: (To Dr. B.) He shuts down.

Dr. B.:   Ralph, can you pinpoint what Clara says or what she does before you feel the tenseness?

Ralph: I guess it is her body language.

Dr. B.:   What specifically acts like a trigger for you?

Ralph: Her lips get tight and drawn back. Her voice gets very soft, and she holds her head to one side (Ralph demonstrates Clara's behavior).

Dr. B.:   Ralph, what is your interpretation of that behavior?

Ralph: She is about to get very upset.

Dr. B.:   Clara, what are your thoughts?

Clara: I do tend to speak softly when something is bothering me, but I'm not aware of the other behaviors.

Dr. B.:   I would like both of you to discuss what happens between you at such times. If we have a better understanding of what is going on, we may be able to work on changing the sequence of events and the outcome.

Clara: Where should we start?

Dr. B.:   Try to recall the most recent event where this process unfolded.

Ralph: I think it happened, for me, the night you got the telephone call from Rhonda about her surgery.

Clara: Yes, I remember. That is an excellent example.

Dr. B.:   Ralph, what is your recollection?

Ralph: Well, I heard Clara talking to Rhonda, and when she got off the phone, she came into the living room, and I could see she was upset.

Dr. B.:   Clara, what is your memory of that event?

Clara: Yes, I was worried. Rhonda told me she had to have some surgery. I wanted to talk about my feelings with Ralph so I went into the living room. Ralph was reading the newspaper. I remember saying that Rhonda had to go into the hospital. I looked at Ralph, but he said nothing.

Dr. B.:   Ralph, can you tell Clara what was happening with you at that time when she came into the living room?

Ralph: (Looks at Clara) As soon as I saw the look on your face, I knew you were going to get upset, and I guess the "Oh, no, here it comes again" thought went through my head.

Clara: And when I tried to talk to you, you were silent.

Ralph: Yes. I was silent. I really didn't know what you wanted me to say or to do, so I just sat there and listened to you.

Clara: Ralph, you said you were listening, but you did not seem to be receptive to me at all. You sat there with this blank look on your face.

Dr. B.:   Ralph, do you remember what you were feeling when Clara told you about Rhonda's surgery.

Ralph: Yes, I think so.

Dr. B.:   Would you mind telling Clara, right now, what you were feeling at that time?

Ralph: (To Clara) I felt terrible. I felt bad for Rhonda. She is such an upbeat person, and I felt so bad that she was going to have to go through that process.

Dr. B.:   (To Ralph) Ralph, would you mind telling Clara how you felt about her when she told you about Rhonda?

Ralph: (To Clara) I felt very sorry for you. I know how close you are to Rhonda. I wished I could have done something to help you and Rhonda.

Clara: (In a soft voice to Ralph) Why couldn't you say this to me that night? It would have been so good for me to hear you say these things to me then—when I really needed your support.

Ralph: I don't know. I guess I didn't think that saying what I was feeling would help you. It might only make things worse. I was afraid you might get even more upset, and then I would feel guilty.

Emotional reactivity frequently interferes with an individual's ability to develop and sustain successful intimate relationships. Emotional reactivity is often seen in individuals who have not completed the developmental process tasks of psychological and emotional differentiation. In the normal course of human development, intellectual functions become differentiated and a separating out of the various emotions and emotional states takes place. As the person matures, thought processes tend to become less influenced by feelings and emotions, and an individual's actions become less impulse driven. Many individuals who enter counseling and psychotherapy, however, have not successfully completed this differentiation process, in the sense that rational thinking and judgment are still influenced by their emotions, and their behavior may be driven more by impulse than by reason.

In the above example, the therapist begins to help Ralph achieve greater degrees of psychological and emotional differentiation by using an intervention technique specifically designed for this purpose. The first step in this process is to teach Ralph how to identify the physiological reactions that serve as preconscious stimulus cues for responding with a specific emotion. Next, Ralph is asked to consider his internal dialogue, because what Ralph says to himself will determine how he responds to his emotional arousal. Individuals differ considerably in their ability to bring into conscious awareness what thoughts trigger emotional reactions and how their self-statements direct their behaviors. Fortunately, Ralph was able to identify his "Oh, no, here it comes" self-talk as being a prelude to his becoming silent. Once these self-statements are identified, a rewriting of the internal dialogue can take place and more desirable behavioral responses can be substituted.

In the next excerpt, this cognitive restructuring process is demonstrated.

Dr. B.: (After a period of silence, Dr. B. addresses the couple.) I would like to help you learn how to deal with these types of situations in a way that would be more satisfying for both of you in the future—a way that would increase your feelings of intimacy.

Clara: That would be wonderful.

Ralph: Yes, that would be good.

Dr. B.: I'd like to return to the discussion you had on the night Rhonda told you about her surgery.

Ralph: O.K.

Clara: That's fine.

Dr. B.: Ralph, I would like you to try something different the next time you find yourself responding to Clara with feelings of tenseness.

Ralph: What should I do?

Dr. B.: Well, as soon as you become aware of your tenseness, I'd like you to say something different to yourself. Usually, you say "Oh, no, here it comes again" or something along those lines—right?

Ralph: Yes.

Dr. B.: Well, what could you say to yourself that would lead to a different behavioral outcome? What could you say to yourself that would prevent you from shutting down or remaining silent?

Ralph: I don't know. What do you suggest?

Dr. B.: Ralph, it is very important for *you* to come up with a self-statement that works for you. Use your own words. What might you say at these times?

Ralph: I could say "Relax" or "Don't run away." I guess, I could say "Be calm" or something.

Dr. B.: Which self-statement would work best for you?

Ralph: I think "Be calm" would be the best one.

Dr. B.: If you were to say "Be calm" would you be able to take your own advice?

Ralph: (Laughing) I think so.

Dr. B.: Good. Then what could you say to yourself that would enable you to connect with Clara in a more supportive and intimate way?

Ralph: Well, maybe I could say "Be calm, Ralph, and listen" and then I could ask Clara to tell me what was on her mind—you know—what she was upset about.

Dr. B.: Clara, what do you think of Ralph's suggestion?

Clara: I like it. I would like it too, Ralph, if when I'm through telling you how I feel, if you would tell me your feelings also. Like you did when Dr. B. asked you how you were feeling about me and Rhonda.

Ralph: This seems so simple. I can do this.

Dr. B.: Sometimes small changes can produce significant effects.

Ralph: What do you mean?

Dr. B.: If you think of your relationship with Clara as a system, any change in one of you will require a change in the other.

Ralph: Sort of an action–reaction idea.

Dr. B.: Exactly, but a person's reaction cannot be predicted so it is important for both people to plan for the change together. (Turning to Clara) Clara, Ralph has agreed to make some changes. He will ask you to tell him what is upsetting you, and you have asked him to express his feelings for you.

Clara: Yes.

Dr. B.: Ralph, how would you like Clara to respond to you at these times?

Ralph: I'm not sure. We've never tried this before.

Clara: Ralph, how would it be if I hugged you and said "thank you" or something like that?

Ralph: That would be fine.

Clara: And maybe we could cuddle for a few minutes?

Ralph: Sure, that would be fine with me.

The enhancing intimacy techniques demonstrated in this and the previous chapters are derived from educational skills training approaches and cognitive behavioral models of relationship enrichment and enhancement. Psychoanalytically trained readers are no doubt aware of the transferential dynamics that surfaced periodically as the therapist worked with Clara and Ralph. For example, Clara's request for Ralph's support during times of crisis were transferentially interpreted by him as her being indecisive and dependent like his mother. Similarly, Clara's fearful belief that Ralph was expecting her to live her life in order to please him was also a transferential distortion. The therapist, however, deliberately chose not to focus on or interpret these transferential distortions to the couple even when Ralph and Clara provided openings for such discussions. Transferential reactions are a part of the human condition. They can be expected to surface, from time to time, in all intimate relationships. Some of these reactions are positive and some of them are negative. They become problematic, however, when transferential distortions and dysfunctional behavioral patterns begin to characterize and dominate a couple's relationship. Working through and resolving serious and problematic transferential distortions with couples is not an objective of this program. Therapists who begin this program with couples and later find that serious transferential distortions are hampering progress should consider discontinuing enrichment work until such transferential distortions are resolved through more traditional marital therapy approaches designed to treat such relationship dynamics.

The cognitive restructuring techniques used in this program and demonstrated with Ralph in the previous example can only be employed successfully when transferential distortions are mild enough to permit a cognitive override of one's emotional reaction. The cognitive restructuring technique can be broken down into five discrete steps.

The first step in the process is to help the person become aware of and identify specific behaviors that his or her partner exhibits that have become conditioned stimuli, which now evoke a predictable type of pysiological response. The second step is to help the person identify the emotional label that he or she characteristically applies to this physiological response. The third step is usually more difficult than the first two. It requires that the person redirect his or her attention away from feeling to what is happening cognitively. To do this requires a certain degree of self-discipline, self-observation, and objectivity. Some people are able to accomplish this task easily. Others may require a number of trial runs and homework assignments before they are able to move on to the fourth step. The fourth step can be considered a pivotal point in this process of cognitive restructuring. To accomplish this, the person must perform three separate cognitive functions:

1. Identify the self-statements that serve to increase one's negative feelings, attitudes, and distancing behaviors toward one's partner.
2. Generate alternative self-statements that will reduce or eliminate negative emotions and attributions.
3. Select a substitute self-statement that can be used to dissipate the negative emotional reaction. This new statement then becomes the stimulus cue for responding to one's partner in a more positive and intimate way.

The last step in this process also has three components: (a) generating a list of possible positive responses that can be used as substitutes for the characteristic ways of treating one's partner that have caused intimacy problems in the past, (b) selecting the most appropriate response alternative, and (c) following through with the selected alternative behavioral response.

In the next excerpt taken from Clara and Ralph's session, the therapist uses this cognitive behavioral approach to help Clara make complementary adjustments to the changes Ralph has agreed to institute. By doing this with Clara, the therapist helps the system make a smooth recalibration to a higher and more satisfying level of functioning.

Dr. B.:   Clara, how does Ralph behave when you think he is going to "shut down?"

Clara: He gets very quiet and withdraws.

Ralph: Clara, that is not altogether true. I don't withdraw all the time. Sometimes I am just quiet, because I don't know what to say. Sometimes I am thinking and sometimes I am simply listening to you. I think that to say I am withdrawn when I am silent is a mischaracterization that is not only inaccurate, but is unfair.

Clara: Well, that's how it feels.

Ralph: That may be how it feels, but it still is not true. Dr. B. taught us to be aware of our interpretations of each other's behaviors and motives. I think this happens a lot. We both do it, but in this case, you are attributing meanings to my silences that are really overgeneralizations. They just don't apply all the time.

Clara: Yes, you are right. I tend to overgeneralize. I know that's not fair.

Dr. B.:   Clara, are you aware of what feelings you experience when Ralph becomes quiet?

Clara: There are several.

Dr. B.:   Can you recall any predictable sequence of feelings?

Clara: Well, I guess first I get anxious and then I get frustrated.

Dr. B.:   So, when Ralph becomes silent, you get anxious and then frustrated.

Clara: Yes.

Ralph: (To Dr. B.) And then she gets angry and then, sometimes, she withdraws. She walks away or walks out of the room.

Clara: Yes, I do get angry sometimes, and I do walk away, but mostly I feel anxious, then frustrated, and sometimes sad.

Dr. B.:   Clara, are you aware of what you say to yourself when you feel your anxiety building?

Clara: My first thought is, "He's withdrawing from me."

Dr. B.:   What happens frequently between people who are intimately involved is that they tend to assume cause-and-effect relationships that are really not valid all the time.

Clara: What do you mean?

Dr. B.:   When Ralph becomes silent, you believe that his behavior signals that a "shutdown" is about to take place.

Clara: Yes.

Dr. B.:   Ralph has said that his silence sometimes precedes a "shutdown," but it can also lead to his thinking about what you are saying. It can also lead to his listening to you intently.

Clara: Yes, Ralph did say those things.

Dr. B.:   On the surface, at the behavioral level, do all Ralph's silences look the same to you, Clara?

Clara: Pretty much. Yes, I'd say they pretty much do.

Dr. B.:   Are there times when Ralph is silent that you don't think a "shutdown" is about to happen?

Clara: Well, when he is reading or watching television, I don't see his behavior as leading to a "shutdown." When he listens to music, I don't think he is going to "shutdown." It is how he relaxes. Sometimes he sits quietly in a chair or on the sofa, and I know he is thinking. He's not "shutting down" then. I guess I only think a "shutdown" happens when we are talking about something important.

Dr. B.:   As far as you can determine, Clara, "shutdowns" occur during important conversations, but not in other contexts?

Clara: I think that's accurate.

Dr. B.:   I guess, then, that this is when the faulty cause-and-effect relationship is most likely to occur.

Clara: Yes, I think so.

Dr. B.:   Sometimes different causes produce the same effect and sometimes the same causes have different effects. Sometimes silences lead to "shutdowns" and other times they don't—even though on the surface they appear the same.

Clara: I never thought of it that way. I never looked at it like that.

Dr. B.:   Clara, would you like to try the technique of saying something different to yourself whenever you become anxious in your talks with

Ralph—you know, like Ralph has agreed to do when he begins to notice his tenseness and before he can think "Oh, no, here it comes again?"

Clara: I can certainly try. Yes, I'd like to do that.

Dr. B.: O.K. Clara, what can you say to yourself when you feel anxious in response to Ralph's silence?

Clara: Well, I can also tell myself to "Be calm."

Dr. B.: Will that work for you?

Clara: Yes, I think so. I have practiced Yoga in the past. I think that can work for me—just saying "Be calm." Then I can use my breathing exercises too. I think that will help also.

Dr. B.: Clara, what can you say to yourself once you have become relaxed?

Clara: I think I can say "Ralph is quiet, but that doesn't mean he's shutting down."

Dr. B.: Then what can you do that will bring about a different outcome for you and Ralph?

Clara: What do you mean by a different outcome?

Dr. B.: If I am not mistaken, in the past when Ralph has become silent, you would get anxious and frustrated, then angry, right?

Clara: Yes.

Dr. B.: Then you might withdraw or even walk away from Ralph.

Clara: Yes.

Dr. B.: The result of this reaction was more distance between you, not an increase of closeness or intimacy. Am I correct?

Clara: Yes.

Dr. B.: Now, with this new approach, you are calm and you have said to yourself "Ralph is quiet, but that doesn't mean that he is shutting down."

Clara: Yes.

Dr. B.: What do you think would be a good behavioral follow-up to this new self-talk? What could you *do* to bring about some type of intimate connection with Ralph?

Clara: I guess I could ask for his support. I could ask him to listen to me and to give me feedback. I think that if I knew Ralph is being attentive and is listening to me, that's really all I want.

Dr. B.: Ralph, what are your thoughts about Clara's new way of approaching you?

Ralph: I like it. I think if you (to Clara) came up to me and told me you wanted me to listen to you, I might not even get tense.

In the above example, two types of interventions are demonstrated. In the first, the therapist teaches Clara (as he taught Ralph) how to edit her internal dialogue so that she can begin to approach Ralph in a way that makes intimate exchanges between them more likely when sensitive issues surface. The second is a reframe designed to effect the couple system.

It is presented casually and takes the form of an innocuous discussion of cause-and-effect relationships. The complex concepts of equifinality (the assumption that an effect or outcome is always produced by the same cause. When a person has this linear causal view, he or she cannot appreciate that a cause can produce a variety of different outcomes) and equipotentiality (the understanding and appreciation that very different causes or antecedents can produce identical effects or outcomes) are explained to Ralph and Clara in a way that can be easily understood. However, understanding these concepts makes it impossible for Clara to interpret all Ralph's silences as "shutdowns" in the future. Similarly, Ralph would be less likely in the future to make strict cause-and-effect assumptions about Clara's behavior.

Sexual Intimacy: Special Considerations

☐ Overview

- Sexual intimacy: Clara and Ralph continued
- Needs strengths differences and differences in desire levels
- Low desire level: Common causes
- History of Sexual Desire Questionnaire
- Education/enrichment vs. sex therapy: Some considerations
- Factors and circumstances that may mask desire discrepancies between partners
- Enhancing sexual intimacy: Key elements in a five-step approach
- Some myths about sexual intimacy and the linear view of sexual behavior
- Sensate focus as a technique for disrupting the linear view of sexual behavior and for enhancing sexual intimacy

Sexual intimacy is a complex issue that deserves special attention, because dissatisfactions in this area often affect all other aspects of a couple's relationship. For this reason, a separate chapter is devoted to this component need. In the author's work over the years, sexual intimacy has been found to be the most sensitive and difficult area to deal with for many couples. The first consideration for a therapist when approaching this area of intimacy is whether the couple's dissatisfactions can be addressed within the context of an educational, enrichment and skills training program such as the one described in this volume, or whether the difficulties are severe enough to warrant a referral to a sex therapist. Some guidelines for making this determination are discussed below.

☐ Differences in Needs Strengths and Differences in Desire Levels

Differences in needs strengths levels are easily identified by comparing the Intimacy Needs Survey scores on this dimension for a given couple. If both partners' needs strengths scores are roughly the same for this component need, needs discrepancy can be ruled out as the major source of dissatisfaction. However, if major needs strengths discrepancies are found to exist, the therapist must explore (a) whether the discrepancy is limited to only this particular component need, (b) whether sexual intimacy represents only one of several component needs where significantly large discrepancies exist, or (c) whether the observed discrepancy in this area of intimacy is reflective of a significantly large difference in Total Needs Strengths scores between the partners.

As is the case with any component need where Reciprocity and/or Receptivity dissatisfactions are present, the extent of dissatisfaction must be taken into account before an appropriate course of action can be plotted. Here again, the therapist must consider those dissatisfactions within the broader context of the couple's relationship, namely, the severity of marital distress and the extent to which the relationship is perceived to be nonvoluntary by the partners.

Next, the therapist must determine whether the observed needs strengths discrepancy reflects a real difference in the needs strengths between the partners or whether the discrepancy represents a change in one's attraction to or desire for his or her mate. In order to make this determination, the therapist should begin by asking the partners to recall when they first noticed a difference in their desire for sexual intercourse. If the partners agree that there has always been a difference in their desire levels, a true need discrepancy may exist. When this is the case, the therapist's role is to help the spouses find ways to meet their sexual needs in a manner acceptable to both partners.

In work with couples who present with desire discrepancies, the author has found that low, reduced, or inhibited sexual desire in one of the partners is the most frequently cited cause of concern. There are a number of reasons for this condition. These are discussed in the next section.

☐ Low Sexual Desire: Common Causes

Low sexual desire that is characteristic for an individual may stem from a variety of sources. For example, there are a number of sex chromosome disorders linked to low sex drive, such as Klinefelter's syndrome in men and Turner's syndrome in women. In men with Klinefelter's syndrome, testicular development is stunted because of the chromosomal aberration and as a result, testosterone production is severely limited. Sperm production may be non-existent or grossly diminished. Men with this condition are not at all troubled by their lack of sexual desire and do not consider it to be a problem. When Personal Sexual Histories are taken from men with Klinefelter's syndrome, it is common to find that they rarely masturbated as teenagers or as adults, had few spontaneously occurring sexual fantasies, were not sexually aroused by watching erotic films, and were not sexually stimulated by reading sexually explicit material. These men do not seek out persons or situations that would be considered sexually arousing and stimulating.

Women with Turner's syndrome do not develop normal ovaries, and, as a result, estrogen production is absent. They do not have spontaneous menstruation or breast development during adolescence. However, since these women do produce adequate levels of testosterone and other related androgens, they do experience low levels of sexual desire. In the majority of cases of Turner's syndrome, women are diagnosed during childhood or adolescence; therefore, breast development can be stimulated by estrogen replacement. Since women with this condition tend to be sexually responsive to their partners, desire discrepancy problems may only come to light if the men with whom they are involved have extremely high needs for sexual intimacy and sexual intercourse.

Whenever there is a history of low sexual desire, medical conditions must first be ruled out as a possible cause. There are a number of medical conditions that can cause a loss of sexual desire in addition to Klinefelter's and Turner's syndromes. These are Addison's disease, severe anemia, chronic active hepatitis, chronic kidney failure, cirrhosis, congestive heart failure, Cushing's syndrome, excessive prolactin secretion, feminizing tumors in men, hemochromatosis, hypothyroidism, Kallmann's syndrome, multiple sclerosis, myotonic diptrophy, Parkinson's disease, pituitary insufficiency, pituitary tumors, testosterone deficiency, and tuberculosis. Certain drugs that are prescribed for medical conditions also can have a negative effect upon sexual desire levels, and for men, the ability to achieve and/or sustain an erection—for example, antiandrogens and antihypertensive medications. In some cases, certain psychotropic medicines can cause desire levels to fall, and with prolonged use, some may cause sterility and impotence. Chronic alcoholism and drug addiction also affect sexual desire. Finally, certain emotional states, such as depression and anxiety, as well as certain types of personality disorders and psychiatric conditions, also affect desire levels.

Large discrepancies in the desire for sexual intercourse and the need for sexual intimacy are often reflected in high levels of relationship dissatisfaction for the partner with the stronger desire and need. Typically, such couples are not good candidates for a skills enhancement and enrichment program. However, sometimes the partner with the stronger sexual need may not report significant levels of relationship distress or dissatisfaction because other factors, circumstances, needs, etc., play a more important role in determining satisfaction for that person. If, however, a substantial decrease in the desire for sexual intercourse and/or the need for sexual intimacy is reported by one or both partners in a relationship where no desire discrepancy existed previously, the therapist must take the time to investigate the possible causes for this decrease. When this is the case, the therapist should schedule separate individual interviews with each partner so that a thorough History of Sexual Desire can be gathered. Since the material collected during these interviews is highly sensitive, the therapist must assure both partners that any information disclosed during the process will remain confidential. It will not be brought into the couple's sessions by the therapist unless the individual decides to share this information with his or her partner. A suggested outline for conducting a History of Sexual Desire is presented below. The first group of questions is designed for the individual whose desire level has decreased. The second group of questions is designed for the partner whose desire for intercourse and need for sexual intimacy has remained the same.

☐ The History of Sexual Desire Questionnaire

Part I

1. When were you first aware that there was a decrease in your desire for sexual intercourse with your partner and/or a decrease in your need for sexual intimacy?
2. Were you the first person to notice this decrease or was it your partner who brought it to your attention?
3. On a scale of 1 to 10, with "1" representing "Not At All Concerned" and "10" representing "Extremely Concerned," how concerned are you about the decrease in your desire for intercourse and/or need for sexual intimacy with your partner?

4. What do you think is responsible for the decrease in your desire for sexual intercourse and need for sexual intimacy?
5. Are you aware of any medical condition, illness, physical ailment, etc., that might be responsible for this decrease?
6. How long has it been since your last physical examination?
7. Are you currently taking any prescribed medications that might have an effect upon your sexual desire?
8. Are you currently taking any over-the-counter medications that might be affecting your desire for sexual intercourse or sexual intimacy?
9. Are you currently using any illicit drugs or alcohol that you believe affect your sexual desire or need for sexual intimacy?
10. Have you ever had this problem in the past? If yes:
    (a) When did it first occur?
    (b) How frequently throughout your life has it occurred?
    (c) How long did the episode (or episodes) last?
    (d) Was it relationship specific or global?
    (e) Was it situationally specific or general?
    (f) What happened to cause your desire for sexual intercourse and need for sexual intimacy to return to normal/original levels?
11. Is the decrease specific to your relationship with your partner or does it represent a general loss of sexual interest and need?
12. Are there any other areas of your life where you are experiencing a loss of interest? If so, describe.
13. If the reduction or loss of desire and need for sexual intimacy is a global one, or if there is a general loss of interest throughout your life, emotional factors must be explored, such as:
    (a) Are you depressed, anxious, or angry?
    (b) Are you unduly stressed?
    (c) Are there difficulties at work that may be causing you concern?
    (d) Have there been any major life circumstance changes?
    (e) Have there been any changes in your physical appearance that may affect your perceptions of yourself as a sexually attractive person?
14. If the reduction or loss of desire for intercourse and need for sexual intimacy is specific to your partner, relationship factors must be explored. The following issues should be considered:
    (a) Have you lost interest in your partner because he or she has become involved in another sexual relationship?
    (b) Are you angry with your partner, and is that anger inhibiting your sexual desire and need for sexual intimacy with that partner?
    (c) Have there been any changes in your partner's physical appear-

ance, attitudes, behaviors, etc., that have made him or her seem less attractive or unattractive?

(d) For any reason, have the sexual relations become painful, distasteful, or repulsive?

(e) Has anything happened in the relationship that has caused you to mistrust your partner?

(f) Has sex become boring, dull, routine, etc.?

15. What has been done to correct the problem?
16. What has been helpful?
17. What has not been helpful?

Part II

1. When were you first aware that there was a decrease in your partner's desire for sexual intercourse or a decrease in his or her need for sexual intimacy with you?
2. On a scale of 1 to 10, with "1" representing "Not At All Concerned" and "10" representing "Extremely Concerned," how concerned are you about the decrease in your partner's sexual desire and need for sexual intimacy?
3. How has the decrease affected your relationship with your partner?
4. How do you feel about this situation?
5. What do you think is responsible for this decrease?
6. How frequently has this problem occurred in your relationship with your partner?
7. Have you ever experienced a similar problem in any of your previous relationships?
8. What did you do to correct this problem?
9. What was helpful?
10. What was not helpful?

Once these interviews are completed, the therapist will be in a position to determine whether the decrease in the desire for sexual intercourse and the need for sexual intimacy can be adequately addressed by using an educational/enrichment format or whether a more intensive therapeutic approach is in order.

There are a number of clear-cut circumstances where education/enrichment would *not* be appropriate. For example:

1. When the symptomatic partner is not distressed by the decrease and reports little or no concern about the problem, but his or her partner is very distressed and registers extreme concern.
2. When the decrease is caused by substance abuse or alcoholism.

3. When there is a long history of fluctuations in the desire for sexual intercourse and need for sexual intimacy.
4. When the loss or reduction of sexual desire is only one of many relationship problems reported by the partner.
5. When the loss of desire is not relationship specific, especially if there is a loss of interest that extends to other areas of the person's life.
6. When the person is involved in another/extramarital relationship.
7. When a partner loses desire for his or her mate because that person has become violent, addicted, unfaithful, or otherwise untrustworthy.
8. When the person is required to perform sexual acts by his or her partner that are deemed to be degrading, repulsive, sinful, etc.

When there is a long-standing history of fluctuations in the desire for sexual intercourse and the need for sexual intimacy, the therapist may decide to investigate the matter more thoroughly by conducting a Personal Sexual History. Guidelines for conducting a Personal Sexual History are presented in Appendix B. In-depth analyses of low and inhibited sexual desire can be facilitated by the use of several assessment tools, for example, Hurlbert Index of Sexual Desire (Apt & Hurlbert, 1992); Sexual Desire Inventory (Spector, Carey, & Steinberg, 1996); and Inhibited Sexual Desire Questionnaire (Masters, Johnson, & Kolodny, 1994).

☐ Desire Discrepancy and Sexual Intimacy Differences

Couples who have a long-standing history of desire discrepancy and differences in need for sexual intimacy still might be able to benefit from an instructional skills training and enrichment program such as the one described in this volume, provided that these differences have not been a source of conflict for the couple and the partners continue to enjoy a warm and loving relationship. Here again, the therapist's judgment (aided by some empirical measures of marital/relationship quality and satisfaction) becomes important in determining a couple's suitability. How partners respond to a few simple questions can be very enlightening. For example:

1. Were you aware of the significant differences in your desire for sexual intercourse and your needs for sexual intimacy before you decided to marry/have a committed relationship?
2. If you were not aware that there were substantial differences in your desires for intercourse and sexual intimacy, how long after you married/became committed did you realize these differences?

3. If you were both aware of these differences before you married/became committed did they ever become a source of conflict between you?
4. If these differences did become a source of conflict between you, were you able to resolve this conflict in a way that was satisfactory for you and for your partner? Explain.
5. Were both of you satisfied with the frequency of sexual intercourse and were your needs for sexual intimacy satisfied as a result of how you resolved this conflict? Explain.
6. If you were unable to resolve this conflict prior to getting married/becoming committed, why did you decide to marry/become committed?
7. How did you think leaving this conflict unresolved would affect your marriage/relationship in the future? Explain.

☐ Factors and Circumstances that May Mask Desire Discrepancies

Sometimes a significant desire discrepancy and need for sexual intimacy does not become apparent until after the couple has married or until after a committed couple has been together for a considerable period of time. There are a number of reasons for such occurrences. For example:

1. During courtship or during the early years of a committed relationship, the partner with an average desire for sexual intercourse and need for sexual intimacy may be more active sexually and very responsive to his or her strong desire/high need mate. However, that partner's true desire and need may surface once the couple has passed through the romantic phase of relationship development.
2. Sometimes there is deliberate deception. This occurs when a partner with average or low desire and need for sexual intimacy engages in uncharacteristically high levels of sexual activity in order to attract a prospective spouse. Once married, that partner's true desire and need become evident, causing considerable marital difficulties.
3. In some instances, women with average desire and need levels marry strong desire/high need men because they want to have children, and strong desire/high need males will engage in intercourse frequently. However, once the desired number of children has been reached, the woman's true desire level and need for sexual intimacy emerges, causing considerable conflict in the relationship.
4. Since women and men reach their sexual peaks at very different times during their lives, a woman's true desire for sexual intercourse, or-

gasm, and sexual intimacy may not emerge until she is in her late 30's or early 40's. By the time a man is 40, in most cases, his desire for sexual intercourse, need for orgasm, and need for sexual intimacy have decreased considerably. Women who discover that they have very strong sexual needs in their late 30's and early 40's may find their partner's (who may be their contemporaries in age or older) diminished desire for intercourse and need for sexual intimacy extremely frustrating.

5. Sometimes, what first appears to be a strong desire for sexual intercourse and a strong need for sexual intimacy actually represents a compulsive sexual disorder. Individuals with such a disorder are preoccupied not with a need to satisfy a normal biological drive but with a need to avoid intense psychic pain. In the most severe cases, according to Masters et al. (1994), the compulsive urge is so intense and unrelenting that it takes the form of ritualistic enactments. If no sexual partner is available, the person will engage in compulsive masturbation. For some individuals, once a day acting out of the compulsive ritual is not sufficient to bring about relief from the overwhelming anxiety, depression, dread, guilt, shame, etc., that plague the person.

It is essential for the therapist to be able to distinguish normal individuals with strong sexual desires and needs from individuals who have a compulsive sexual disorder. Taking a thorough Personal Sexual History is recommended whenever the therapist suspects that a partner suffers from a compulsive sexual disorder. If, upon completion of the Personal Sexual History, the therapist is still unsure of whether the person has a compulsive sexual disorder, a referral to a sex therapist should be made.

☐ A Systematic Approach to Enhancing Sexual Intimacy

Once couples have been successful in their attempts to increase intimacy satisfactions in other less sensitive component needs areas of intimacy, they are ready, in most cases, to focus on the sexual dimension of their relationship. Over the years, the author has found that most couples require a certain amount of guidance and structure when working on issues of sexual intimacy. As a result, a systematic approach was developed to facilitate couples' work in this component need area. The key elements of this approach include:

1. The completion of a *Sexual Attitudes and Practices Questionnaire* (Appendix C).

2. Identification of the sexual issues that are of concern.
3. Discussion of these issues.
4. Assigning relevant homework exercises.
5. Evaluating program success.

To illustrate this five-step approach, let us return to Clara and Ralph.

Dr. B.: Good afternoon folks.

Clara: Good afternoon, Dr. B.

Ralph: Nice to see you again, Doc.

Dr. B.: Well, you have done very well with the Emotional, the Psychological and the Social and Recreational areas of intimacy as far as I can determine. Are there any issues remaining, in these areas, that either of you believes still require attention before we move on to the remaining two dimensions of intimacy?

Ralph: No, I'm O.K. with them.

Clara: Me too.

Dr. B.: The two remaining areas of concern are Physical and Sexual intimacy.

Ralph: Yes.

Clara: Yes.

Dr. B.: In your case, I think it is appropriate to treat these two issues together, because of something that Clara said when we reviewed the results from the Intimacy Needs Survey.

Clara: What was that?

Dr. B.: If my memory serves me correctly, I believe you said that some of the tenderness and the nonsexual physical aspects of your relationship with Ralph had declined.

Clara: Yes, that was true when I said it at the beginning, but it seems to have gotten a little better since we have been coming here.

Dr. B.: Good to hear.

Clara: But, we still can use some improvement in this area as far as I'm concerned.

Dr. B.: Yes, I also recall that you said you would like Ralph to be physically intimate with you from time to time without this physical intimacy always leading to something sexual.

Clara: Yes, this is still the case. Even though Ralph has become more tender (turns to Ralph) I'd still like some cuddle time without it turning into something sexual.

Ralph: I know, but since we have not been having sex as much now as we've had in the past, whenever we hug or kiss or have close body contact in bed, I get turned on. Clara, you know how turned on to you I've always been.

Clara: Yes, I know Ralph, and I am still turned on to you, but the other, nonsexual stuff is still important.

Dr. B.:   Clara, I wonder if this could be why you said earlier in these sessions that you sometimes feel like a sexual object?

Clara: Precisely. I know Ralph does not see me that way, but sometimes it feels like it.

Dr. B.:   What you two are experiencing is a very common occurrence and there are some very simple exercises you can do together that can help you overcome this problem.

Ralph: You know, Dr. B., you make everything seem so simple. It seems that you have an exercise or a homework assignment for just about any problem (laughs).

Clara: Yes, Ralph and I joke about you sometimes. Sometimes we even joke about you with our friends. We'll say to our friends sometimes when a problem arises, "Dr. B. probably has an exercise for that" (laughs).

Dr. B.:   Well, I wish I did have an exercise or an assignment for everything (laughing), but it just ain't so. However, you are an easy couple to work with. You are eager to learn and very receptive, and in spite of some minor difficulties, you have a very solid relationship. What seems to be a simple exercise or solution for you may be extremely difficult for couples whose relationship is seriously distressed.

Clara: I guess that's true.

Dr. B.:   Before I give you your next homework assignment (laughs), I would like you to privately complete the *Sexual Attitudes and Practices Questionnaire*. Unlike the other questionnaires I have asked you to complete, you do not have to share your responses with each other unless you feel comfortable doing so. The only person who will see your responses to these questions will be me, and I will not introduce anything from these questionnaires into the sessions. However, if there is an issue on your own questionnaire that you would like to discuss, you may bring it up for discussion. If you are uncomfortable discussing any issue in my presence then you can discuss that issue in the privacy of your own home, using the communication skills you have learned here. Do you have any questions before I give these forms to you?

Clara: No.

Ralph: None, no questions.

☐ Myths about Sexual Intimacy and the Linear Views of Sexual Behavior

It is often helpful to treat Physical intimacy within the context of Sexual intimacy so that a clear distinction can be made between these two types of intimate experiences and behaviors. Clara's complaint about Ralph's tendency to view all physically intimate contact as a prelude to some form of sexual behavior is a fairly common one. In clinical work, one frequently comes across men who are genuinely surprised to see Sexual intimacy and Physical intimacy treated as separate and distinct component needs in the Intimacy Needs Survey. For some men, the notion that there are other forms of intimacy which are not sexual in nature, is a completely novel idea. Although Ralph does not fall into this category, he does represent a group of men who have some difficulty separating sexual intimacy from physical intimacy. Such men frequently have a linear view when it comes to sexual behavior, namely, that any physical interaction with a woman that the man considers to be of a sexual nature must culminate in sexual intercourse and orgasm. Disrupting this linear progression of physical affection → sexual foreplay → intercourse → orgasm— with men who have this orientation is crucial for increasing intimacy in both the physical and sexual realms of interaction with their partners. A strategy for breaking this pattern is employed with Ralph and Clara.

Dr. B.:   Well, that didn't take too long.

Clara: (Handing Dr. B. her Sexual Attitudes and Practices Questionnaire) No, it didn't, but the first part of the questionnaire got me thinking about several things that I had not considered before.

Ralph: (Handing Dr. B. his Sexual Attitudes and Practices Questionnaire) Yes, it did get me thinking about some things I had never given much thought to.

Dr. B.:   (Looks over the questionnaires first and then asks) O.K., how would you like to proceed now?

Clara: I don't mind if Ralph looks at my questionnaire. There is nothing on this form, you know—my answers, that I can't share with Ralph.

Ralph: Same here. I am also a little curious about how Clara answered some of these questions (turns toward Clara). I'd like to know what you consider to be the most sexually attractive physical characteristics I possess?

Clara: Well, there are several things that sort of act in concert to make you physically attractive. Your broad shoulders, your narrow waist and your flat stomach. You also have strong thighs and a cute butt! (Laughs).

Ralph: Thanks. I was just thinking the same about you. Not your broad shoulders and strong thighs (laughs), but your cute butt! (Laughs).

Clara: Anything else?

Ralph: You know. I've told you a million times what beautiful long legs you have, and your breasts are really firm. You know how much I appreciate your figure.

Clara: Thank you, Ralph, but you know I'd like my boobs to be a little bigger. That is kind of you to say.

Ralph: That's not kind. It is the truth. I wouldn't change a thing about your looks and you know that. How did you answer this question about yourself and how did you think I was going to answer it?

Clara: I knew what you would say since we talked about this before.

Ralph: And I knew what you'd say about yourself. I know that you like your legs.

Clara: Yes, they have been an asset to me in a number of ways, not only as attractive, but in my tennis game (laughs).

Ralph: How did you think I would answer the question about my own physical attractiveness?

Clara: Well, I know that you take good care of yourself physically and that your body is a source of pride for you. I thought you'd say your overall body build. Was I right?

Ralph: Yes, right on target.

Clara: O.K. What did you say is the most attractive aspect of my personality? What did you say in response to that question? I really didn't know how you would answer that.

Ralph: Your sense of humor about sexual matters and your complete freedom about yourself sexually.

Clara: I understand about the complete freedom part, but what about my sense of humor in sexual matters. What do you mean?

Ralph: Like the time you surprised me for my birthday by serving dinner in your bikini bra and panties, and the time we planned to go skinny-dipping and you showed up wearing a snorkel and giant rubber webbed feet (laughs). That really cracked me up. There you were butt naked and wearing a snorkel and flippers (laughs).

Clara: (Laughing) Yes, I've done some nutty things, but I've always had a weird sense of humor.

Ralph: It's weird and I love it!

Clara: Thanks.

Ralph: What do you consider to be the sexiest aspect of your personality?

Clara: My intellect, my mind.

Ralph: (Laughing) You know I love you for your mind. That goes without saying. Great legs, a nice butt, and a good mind. An unbeatable combination! Who could ask for anything more?

Clara: (Laughing) Yes! Notice the order. My legs, my butt, then my mind!

Ralph: Sometimes a guy can't win! (Laughs).

Clara: You know I'm only joking. I know you appreciate my mind. I'm just ribbing you.

Ralph: What did you put down for the most sexually attractive aspect of my personality? I didn't know how you would answer that question.

Clara: Your walk.

Ralph: My walk?

Clara: Yes, your walk reflects who you are. It reflects your personality—
at least to me it does. The way you hold yourself when you walk. You have
a way of holding your body that shows self-confidence and assurance. Your
self-confidence is very attractive to me and it really shows in the way you
walk.

Ralph: Thank you. That is a nice thing to say. I've always considered my
sincerity to be something women found attractive. I never saw my self-
confidence as an asset, and I never thought my confidence was reflected in
my walk.

Clara: Well, I think it is very evident.

Ralph: Thanks. That is really nice.

Clara: I thought you would say that your reliability and sincerity were
your most sexually attractive personality traits. I wasn't too far off, was I?

Ralph: No, you weren't.

Putting the Couple at Ease When Discussing Sexual Issues

The questions that appear in Part I of the Sexual Attitudes and Practices
Questionnaire are worded in a way designed to reduce anxiety by high-
lighting the positive aspects of a couple's sexual relationship. Asking each
respondent to consider how his or her partner would answer these same
questions facilitates role taking and perspective reversal and provides a
structured format for discussing the more sexually explicit questions contained in Part II. Sensitivity to the couple's comfort level in dealing with
sexual matters is important. The therapist must be able to recognize when
one or both of the partners is beginning to become uncomfortable. Some
couples, like Clara and Ralph, will be able to use humor to reduce the
initial uneasiness that sometimes develops when sexual material is discussed. Other couples, however, may be more comfortable with an edu-
cational/instructional approach to dealing with this component need area.
Still others may wish to treat sexual matters in a straightforward, matter-
of-fact manner. The therapist must be attuned to the couple's style so that
he or she can follow the couple's lead.

Clara: I'd like to talk a little about question five. Would you be O.K. talking about this, Ralph?

Ralph: Sure. What is question five? (looks at his Sexual Attitudes and
Practices Questionnaire). Oh, your ideal conditions for sex. O.K. That's fine.
Actually, I'd really like to know. What are your ideal conditions for having
good sex?

Clara: Time.

Ralph: Time? Can you explain a little?

Clara: Yes. I need some time to get in the mood. I don't like to feel rushed, either before or after.

Ralph: I didn't think you minded quickies.

Clara: Quickies are fine sometimes, but lately it seems that all we have are quickies.

Dr. B.:   Clara, if you could set the stage for lovemaking, you know, if you were a director on a movie set, how would you have this love scene played out?

Clara: You mean like in my fantasies?

Dr. B.: Yes. Tell Ralph how you envision this scene being played out between you and him.

Clara: Well, it isn't really anything elaborate. It would take place early in the evening after dinner when we've cleaned up the dishes and all.

Dr. B.:   Fine. Go on.

Clara: Well (to Ralph) we would take a shower together and then we would dry each other off and then go into the bedroom and make love. Then after that, we could listen to some music and you would read poetry to me. Then we'd make love again and again.

Ralph: Sounds good to me. We've done that in the past, but it has been a long time since we have taken that much time. I agree, we need to do this kind of thing more often.

Clara: I hope we can.

Dr. B.:   You know, folks, some people think that sex should be spontaneous to be good, but that really isn't the case. That is really one of the many myths about good sex. For many people, planning to have sex and planning a romantic evening often results in a very good sexual experience for both people. For some people, the anticipation can be very stimulating. You may want to think about planning some evenings beforehand—from time to time.

Ralph: I think we could do that.

Clara: I hope we can.

Dr. B.:   Would you like to decide upon some times now, or would you like to discuss some possible times after this session is over?

Clara: I'd rather not use our time here to discuss this. I'd rather talk about it with Ralph later.

Ralph: Yes, this would not be the best use of this time. We can do it later.

Dr. B.:   O.K. Is there anything else on Part I that you would like to focus on?

Clara: No.

Ralph: No. There is nothing on Part I or Part II that I'd like to discuss. I think we both agree on what we like and what we dislike.

Clara: Yes. We pretty much know what we like. Dr. B., you said you had an exercise—a homework assignment—for us that would help us become physically more intimate without it always becoming sexual.

Dr. B.:   Yes.

Clara: Can we talk a little about that before this session is over?

Dr. B.:   Sure. There are sensate focus exercises that you can use in the privacy of your home. Sensate focus was developed by Masters and Johnson as a method that people can use to disrupt the pattern where displays of physical affection lead automatically to sexual foreplay that then ends in intercourse and orgasm. As I said earlier, this is a fairly common problem. I have put together a sensate focus program based upon some sensate focus models developed by several sex therapists. I can give you a copy of these exercises for you to review. We can discuss how to proceed at our next session.

Clara: That sounds good.

Ralph: O.K. with me.

☐ The Use of Sensate Focus in Enhancing Intimacy

Sensate focus exercises are routinely used by sex therapists and educators to help couples enrich their relationship. Sensate focus exercises are very useful in disrupting the linear approach to sexual intercourse that exists in many relationships. These exercises help couples learn how to differentiate between sensual feelings and sexual feelings, thereby allowing them to experience more sensuality in their relationship. Masters and Johnson (1966, 1970) found, quite early in their work, that simply asking couples to practice touching each other in the privacy of their home was not sufficient to help them become more sensual. Masters and Johnson, therefore, developed a step-by-step structured procedure that would help couples achieve greater sensuality, physical pleasure, and sexual intimacy in their relationship. The sensate focus guidelines that appear in Appendix D have been distilled from a variety of sources (Masters & Johnson; Masters et al., 1994; McCarthy & McCarthy, 1984; Zilbergeld, 1992). They outline only the *nongenital* phase of sensate focus that is designed to emphasize sensuality rather than sexuality. During the nongenital touching phase of sensate focus, the couple is required to refrain from engaging in any type of sexual activity on those days that they practice the exercises. Here again, it must be understood that the nongenital sensate focus exercises are assigned to couples where a linear approach to sexual intercourse has been identified as a source of concern. Clearly, Ralph and Clara fall into this category. The more successful Ralph and Clara are in abstaining from sexual contact while engaging in sensate focus, the more successful they will most likely be in disrupting the pattern of linear sexual progression. Later on, Ralph and Clara may wish to complete a second set of sensate focus exercises that emphasize genital touching, pleasuring, and sexual intercourse. These exercises can then become integrated with the nongenital exercises of Phase I, resulting in a much more complete sensual/sexual experience. At this point, however, the goal is to disrupt the linear sexual progression pattern that has characterized their relationship.

8

Final Considerations

☐ Overview

- Final considerations
- Evaluating therapeutic effectiveness by using the Intimacy Needs Survey
- Some beliefs, attitudes, expectations, and misconceptions that serve as impediments to intimacy
- Two fundamental roles of the therapist
- Concluding thoughts

This volume was written to offer clinicians a theory-based, educational, and skills training programmatic approach to help couples who are not seriously distressed learn ways to increase the intimacy they share in their relationships. The degree to which a couple benefits from participating in such an enrichment program can be assessed by comparing each partner's preprogram and postprogram Intimacy Needs Survey scores for Receptivity and Reciprocity satisfaction for those component needs that were initially identified as problematic. Since the need for intimacy appears to be a fairly stable trait-like quality, changes in Component Needs Strengths and Total Needs Strengths should not be expected. One would expect satisfaction percentage scores to increase if the program had been successful. However, caution should be exercised when statistical procedures are used to evaluate outcome effectiveness, because pre-program–post-program changes in Receptivity satisfaction and Reciprocity satisfaction that are not statistically significant may still have great personal significance and meaning for the partners, since intimacy satisfactions are highly subjective.

It should not be assumed that simply because a couple's relationship is not seriously distressed that stumbling blocks to achieving greater intimacy do not exist. Over the years the author has found there to be a number of common beliefs, attitudes, expectations, and misconceptions that people have about what constitutes intimacy and its nature that serve as impediments to achieving greater degrees of intimacy.

Probably the most commonly held misconception about the nature of intimacy is that it is unidimensional. Frequently, the sexual component of intimacy is all that is considered. This misconception is easily dispensed with by having the person complete the Intimacy Needs Survey. Once a person who holds such a unidimensional view of intimacy is asked to complete the Intimacy Needs Survey, a reframing takes place that makes it exceedingly difficult for him or her to maintain the previously held narrow and monolithic perspective. The effect of the Intimacy Needs Survey upon the way a person conceptualizes intimacy is subtle, yet extremely powerful.

Another common misconception that people have about intimacy is to confuse intimacy with knowledge and understanding. The underlying assumption here is that if an individual knows his or her partner well, especially if he or she understands the partner's behaviors and motives, that intimacy exists between them. Sometimes one comes across partners who have been together for years and who really know each other very well. They know each other's likes, dislikes, habits, and idiosyncrasies, but they feel a vague sense of isolation, loneliness, and loss in their relationship, the cause of which they are unable to identify. Frequently, the problem is that the partners are close but they are not intimate. It is not unusual to find this sense of isolation, loneliness, and loss emerging in marriages when the last child is about to leave home or when spouses finally retire. In many instances, core intimacy needs that had been met satisfactorily by children, colleagues, and friends cannot be satisfied by one's partner in a relationship where there has been closeness but little intimacy.

Agreement and sameness are often equated with intimacy by some individuals. When intimacy is conceptualized in this fashion, disagreements and differences tend to cause serious conflicts between partners, since the expectation for sameness and agreement usually extends to all areas of intimacy. For individuals who subscribe to such a view of intimacy, differences pose serious threats to relationship cohesion. Several factors are responsible for the belief that sameness and agreement equal intimacy. The first one is cultural and stems from the romantic ideas of love discussed in Chapter 1. The second is psychological in that the need for sameness and agreement represents a defense against separateness. Typically, an individual who has not successfully separated and individuated from a primary attachment figure and is still enmeshed in his or her family of origin will transfer this dependency onto his or her partner. The illusion of symbiotic interdependency can only be maintained, however, if no differences are acknowledged between the two partners. The third contributing factor can be traced to Biblical teachings and expectations for marriage, for example, the "two shall become one flesh." When religious beliefs and dogma are central to a couple's relationship, agreement between the partners concerning issues of faith, morals, ethics, individual conduct, marital commitments, and family behavior is crucial, and there may be very little room for differences.

The belief that agreement and sameness are the central ingredients of an intimate relationship can be found in many marriages. Regardless of the cause, holding steadfast to such beliefs may actually limit the amount of intimacy a couple can achieve.

In some relationships, differences and disagreements between the partners do not become a source of conflict or threat to the integrity of the relationship, because the partners are able to agree to disagree. Agreeing to disagree in a relationship does not necessarily mean that intimacy will be compromised. Intimacy will only suffer if there is a prohibition against discussing those areas of disagreement with one's partner. When this occurs, communication between the partners may become restricted to neutral topics and nonconflictual areas of the relationship. Essentially, the relationship evolves into one where the partners are compatible but not intimate.

Finally, some people believe that if they love their partners then intimacy automatically exists in their relationship. In Chapter 1, the basic ingredients of mature love (as opposed to romantic/erotic love) were identified. These were (a) in-depth knowledge of one's partner, (b) respect for one's partner, (c) acceptance of the other, and (d) trust and honesty. It is possible for all these qualities to be present in a relationship between two people and for intimacy still not to exist between the partners. What is missing from such relationships is the experiential meeting of selves.

Therapists whose goal is to help couples become more intimate should be aware of these beliefs, attitudes, expectations, and misconceptions about intimacy so that they can be recognized as stumbling blocks to progress. How the therapist tackles these issues is a matter of personal style. The therapist has two fundamental roles throughout the process of therapy: (a) to create a secure environment by being genuine, accepting, and supportive so that the partners can begin to risk being and sharing themselves, and (b) to help the partners acquire the skills that are needed to increase intimacy in their relationship.

☐ Concluding Thoughts

Participation in a program such as the one outlined in this volume is only the first step in the lifelong process of enhancing intimacy. Like anything of value that is worth attaining, considerable work and effort are required to achieve the precious moments of intimacy that sustain us through the more mundane aspects of everyday life and existence. The Enhancing Intimacy Program can show couples the way, but it cannot create or produce intimacy. Intimacy is a two-way street. It requires effort from both directions, from both sides, from both partners. It requires commitment, desire, and the willingness to risk being who we really are; intimacy is scary, exhilarating, and soothing all at the same time. Communication, conflict negotiation, and problem-solving skills can get us halfway there; trust will take us the rest of the way. Life is short, but the time we spend in intimate connections with someone we love is shorter even still. If reading this volume makes it easier for the therapist to help couples become more intimate, then the author will have accomplished his task.

REFERENCES

Adams, J. S. (1963). Inequity in social exchange. In L. Berkowitz (Ed.), *Advances in experimental social psychology, Vol. 2* (pp. 256–270). New York: Academic Press.

Adams, J. S. (1965). Towards an understanding of inequity. *Journal of Abnormal and Social Psychology, 67,* 422–436.

Ainsworth, M. D. S., Blehar, M. C., Waters, E., & Wall, S. (1978). *Patterns of attachment: A psychological study of the strange situation.* Hillside, NJ: Erlbaum.

Apt, C., & Hurlbert, D. F. (1992). Motherhood and female sexuality beyond one year postpartum: A study of military wives. *Journal of Sex Education and Therapy, 18,* 104–114.

Bagarozzi, D. A. (1983). Methodological developments in measuring social exchange perceptions in marital dyads (SIDCARB): A new tool for clinical intervention. In D. A. Bagarozzi, A. P. Jurich, & R. W. Jackson (Eds.), *New perspectives in marital and family therapy: Theory, research and practice* (pp. 48–78). New York: Human Sciences Press.

Bagarozzi, D. A. (1986). Premarital therapy. In F. P. Piercy & D. Sprenkel (Eds.), *Family therapy sourcebook* (pp. 165–188). New York: Guilford.

Bagarozzi, D. A. (1989). Family diagnostic testing: A neglected area of expertise for the family psychologist. *American Journal of Family Therapy, 17,* 257–272.

Bagarozzi, D. A. (1999). Marital intimacy: Assessment and clinical considerations. In J. Carlson & L. Sperry (Eds.), *The intimate couple* (pp. 66–83). Philadelphia: Brunner/Mazel.

Bagarozzi, D. A., & Anderson, S. A. (1989). *Personal, marital and family myths: Theoretical formulations and clinical strategies.* New York: Norton.

Bagarozzi, D. A., & Atilano, R. B. (1982). SIDCARB: A clinical tool for rapid assessment of social exchange inequities and relationship barriers. *Journal of Sex and Marital Therapy, 8,* 325–334.

Bagarozzi, D. A., & Bagarozzi, J. I. (1982). A theoretically derived model of premarital intervention: The making of a family system. *Clinical Social Work Journal, 10,* 52–62.

Bagarozzi, D. A., Bagarozzi, J. I., Anderson, S. A., & Pollane, L. (1984). Premarital education and training sequence (PETS): A three year follow up of an experimental study. *Journal of Counseling and Development, 63,* 91–100.

Bagarozzi, D. A., & Pollane, L. (1983). A replication and validation of the Spousal Inventory of Desired Changes and Relationship Barriers (SIDCARB): Elaborations on diagnostic and clinical utilization. *Journal of Sex and Marital Therapy, 9,* 303–315.

Bagarozzi, D. A., & Wodarski, J. S. (1977). A social exchange typology of conjugal relationships and conflict development. *Journal of Marriage and Family Counseling, 3,* 53–61.

Blood, R. O., & Wolfe, D. M. (1960). *Husbands and wives.* New York: The Free Press.

Bowlby, J. (1969). *Attachment and loss: Vol. I. Attachment.* New York: Basic Books.

Bowlby, J. (1973). *Attachment and loss: Vol. II. Separation.* New York: Basic Books

Bowlby, J. (1979). *The making and breaking of affectional bonds.* New York: Mathuen.

Bowlby, J. (1980). *Attachment and loss: Vol. III. Loss, sadness and depression.* New York: Basic Books.

125

Bowlby, J. (1988). *A secure base.* New York: Basic Books.

Brazelton, T. B., & Cramer, B. G. (1990). *The earliest relationship: Parents, infants and the drama of early attachment.* New York: Addison Wesley.

Carson, R. (1969). *Interaction concepts of personality.* Chicago: Aldine.

Doane, J. I., & Diamond, D. (1994). *Affect and attachment in the family: A family based treatment of major psychiatric disorder.* New York: Basic Books.

Edwards, J. M. (1969). Familial behavior as social exchange. *Journal of Marriage and the Family, 31,* 518–527.

Erikson, E. (1968). *Identity: Youth and crisis.* New York: International Universities Press.

Foa, U. G. (1971). Interpersonal and economic resources. *Science, 171,* 345–351.

Homans, G. (1974). *Social behavior: Its elementary forms* (2nd ed.). New York: Harcourt, Brace and World.

Horner, A. J. (1984). *Object relations and the developing ego in therapy.* Northvale, NJ: Aronson.

L'Abate, L., & Bagarozzi, D. A. (1993). *Sourcebook of marriage and family evaluation.* New York: Brunner/Mazel.

Levinger, G. A. (1976). A social psychological perspective on marital dissolution. *Journal of Social Issues, 32,* 21–47.

Lewis, R. A., & Spanier, G. B. (1979). Theorizing about the quality and stability of marriage. In W. R. Bunn, R. Hill, F. I. Nye, & I. L. Reiss (Eds.), *Contemporary theories about the family,* Vol. 1. London: Free Press.

Maccoby, E., & Masters, J. (1970). Attachment and dependency. In P. H. Mussen (Ed.), *Carmichael's manual of child psychology, Vol. II* (pp. 73–157). New York: Wiley.

Mahler, M., Pine, F., & Bergman, A. (1975). *The psychological birth of the human infant.* New York: Basic Books.

Masters, W. H., & Johnson, V. E. (1966). *Human sexual response.* New York: Little, Brown.

Masters, W. H., & Johnson, V. E. (1970) *Human sexual inadequacy.* Boston: Little, Brown.

Masters, W. A., Johnson, V. E., & Kolodny, R. C. (1994). *Heterosexuality.* New York: Harper.

McCarthy, B., & McCarthy, E. (1984). *Sexual awareness.* New York: Carroll & Graf.

Olson, D. H. (1975). Intimacy and the aging family. In C. S. Hart (Ed.), *Realities of aging.* Minneapolis, MN: University of Minnesota Press.

Olson, D. H. (1977). *Quest for intimacy.* Unpublished manuscript, University of Minnesota.

Shaefer, M. I., & Olson, D. H. (1981). Assessing intimacy: The PAIR Inventory. *Journal of Marital and Family Therapy, 7,* 47–60.

Slade, A., & Arber, L. J. (1992) Attachment, drives and development: Conflicts and convergences in theory. In J. Barron, M. Eagle, & D. Wolitsky (Eds.), *Interface of psychoanalysis and psychology* (pp. 154–185). Washington, DC: APA Publications.

Spector, L. P., Carey, M. P., & Steinberg, L. (1996). The sexual desire inventory: Development, factor structure and evidence of reliability. *Journal of Sex and Marital Therapy, 22,* 175–190.

Sullivan, H. S. (1953). *The interpersonal theory of psychiatry.* New York: W. W. Norton.

Thibaut, J., & Kelley, H. H. (1959). *The social psychology of groups.* New York: Wiley.

Waller, W., & Hill, R. (1951). *The family: A dynamic interpretation.* New York: The Dryden Press.

Zilbergeld, B. (1992). *The new male sexuality.* New York: Bantam Books.

APPENDIX A

Spousal Inventory of Desired Change and Relationship Barriers: SIDCARB

Spousal Inventory of Desired Change and Relationship Barriers: SIDCARB

Date_____   □ Husband   □ Wife

In this section you are asked to think about how satisfied you are with your spouse's behavior in a number of areas of your marriage. Evaluate whether your husband or wife is doing his or her fair share to contribute to the overall satisfaction of the marriage and the degree to which you would like to see changes in his/her behavior in any of the following areas of your relationship.

1 = Little change   4 = Medium change   7 = Great deal of change

	little change ... great deal of change
1. *Household Chores:* Cooking, cleaning, repairs around the house, gardening, shopping, taking out the trash, care of the automobile, pets, etc.	1 2 3 4 5 6 7
2. *Finances:* Amount spouse spends, earns, saves, invests; how well spouse budgets, manages, etc.	1 2 3 4 5 6 7
3. *Communication:* Time spent talking; sharing ideas and feelings; topics discussed; openness; sincerity; listening to you; understanding your ideas, views, feelings, interests, etc.	1 2 3 4 5 6 7
4. *Expression of Love and Affection:* Open expression of love, fondness, appreciation, encouragement, doing special things for you like cooking a favorite meal, buying you presents, noticing your appearance, etc.	1 2 3 4 5 6 7
5. *In-Laws (your parents and his or her parents):* Time spent with them, confiding in them, depending upon them, liking them, interference from them, etc.	1 2 3 4 5 6 7
6. *Religion:* Church/synagogue attendance, religiousness, financial support, involvement, differences of religion, religious instruction of children, celebration of holidays, unkept vows, etc.	1 2 3 4 5 6 7
7. *Recreation:* Time spent together, alone, with friends, vacations together or separate, etc.	1 2 3 4 5 6 7
8. *Sexual Relations:* Frequency, type, duration, contraception, etc.	1 2 3 4 5 6 7
9. *Friendships:* Your spouse's friends, mutual friends, time spouse spends with friends, time you spend with friends, time you both spend with mutual friends, openness of your marriage to outsiders, confidences to friends, etc.	1 2 3 4 5 6 7
10. *Children:* Decision to have children, how many, spacing, adoption, education, sex education, time spent with children by your spouse, as a family, child rearing, management, discipline, etc.	1 2 3 4 5 6 7

	Not at all satisfied						Very Satisfied
11. In general, how satisfied are you with your marriage?	1	2	3	4	5	6	7
12. In general, how satisfied are you with your spouse?	1	2	3	4	5	6	7
13. How committed are you to remaining married?	1	2	3	4	5	6	7

	Not at all						Very often
14. How often have you thought about separation from your spouse in the last six months?	1	2	3	4	5	6	7
15. How often have you thought about divorce in the last six months?	1	2	3	4	5	6	7

In this section you are asked to evaluate your marriage in terms of its overall satisfaction and dissatisfaction. All spouses are dissatisfied with their partners and their marriage at one time or another and thoughts of separation and divorce are universal; that is, all people have these thoughts. Keeping this in mind, please answer the following questions.

	Not at all						Very willing
16. If you were dissatisfied with your spouse, how willing would you be to separate if things did not improve?	1	2	3	4	5	6	7
17. If you were dissatisfied with your spouse, how willing would you be to get a divorce if things did not improve?	1	2	3	4	5	6	7

If your marriage were not satisfying, would any of the following circumstances prevent you from leaving your spouse? How important would each be?

	Not at all important						Very important
18. Obligations to children	1	2	3	4	5	6	7
19. Commitment to marriage vows	1	2	3	4	5	6	7
20. Religious beliefs	1	2	3	4	5	6	7
21. Relatives	1	2	3	4	5	6	7
22. Friends and neighbors	1	2	3	4	5	6	7
23. Job considerations	1	2	3	4	5	6	7
24. Legal considerations	1	2	3	4	5	6	7
25. Financial considerations	1	2	3	4	5	6	7
26. Other (specify)	1	2	3	4	5	6	7

Spousal Inventory of Desired Changes and Relationship Barriers: SIDCARB

SCORING GUIDELINES

I. Factor I
    Score items 1 through 10 as follows:

    Little change   = 1
    A great deal of change = 7

    1, 2, 3, 4, 5, 6, 7, 8, 9, 10 _____ Total raw score

    Score items 11 through 13 as follows:

    Not at all satisfied   = 7
    Very satisfied   = 1
    Not at all committed   = 7
    Very committed   = 1

    11, 12, 13 _____ Total raw score

    Score items 14 and 15 as follows:

    Not at all   = 1
    Very often   = 7

    14, 15 _____ Total raw score

    Factor I _____ Grand total raw score
    Factor I _____ Standard score

II. Factor II
    Score items 16 and 17 as follows:

    Not at all   = 7
    Very willing   = 1

    16, 17 _____ Total raw score

    Score items 18 through 21 as follows:

    Not at all important   = 1
    Very important   = 7

    18, 19, 20, 21 _____ Total raw score

    Factor II _____ Grand total raw score
    Factor II _____ Standard score

III. Factor III
Score items 22 through 25 as follows:

Not at all important   = 1
Very important   = 7

22, 23, 24, 25   _____ Total raw score

                    Factor III _____ Grand total raw score
                    Factor III _____ Standard score

Spousal Inventory of Desired Change and Relationship Barriers: SIDCARB

Factor I

Raw Score	Standard Score	Raw Score	Standard Score
15	37.5	64	68.3
16	38.2	65	68.9
17	39.8	66	69.6
18	39.4	67	70.2
19	40.0	68	70.8
20	40.7	69	71.5
21	41.3	70	72.1
22	41.9	71	72.7
23	42.6	72	73.3
24	43.2	73	74.0
25	43.8	74	74.6
26	44.4	75	75.2
27	45.1	76	75.9
28	45.7	77	76.5
29	46.3	78	77.1
30	46.9	79	77.7
31	47.6	80	78.4
32	48.2	81	79.0
33	48.8	82	79.6
34	49.5	83	80.2
35	50.0	84	80.9
36	51.0	85	81.5
37	51.4	86	82.1
38	52.0	87	82.8
39	52.6	88	83.4
40	53.2	89	84.0
41	53.9	90	84.7
42	54.5	91	85.3
43	55.1	92	85.9
44	55.7	93	86.6
45	56.4	94	87.2
46	57.0	95	87.8
47	57.6	96	88.4
48	58.3	97	89.0
49	58.9	98	89.7
50	59.5	99	90.3
51	60.2	100	90.9
52	60.8	101	91.6
53	61.4	102	92.2
54	62.0	103	92.8
55	62.7	104	93.4
56	63.3	105	94.1
57	63.9		
58	64.6		
59	65.2		
60	65.8		
61	66.4		
62	67.1		
63	67.7		

Spousal Inventory of Desired Change and Relationship Barriers: SIDCARB

Factor II

Raw Score	Standard Score
6	24.6
7	25.8
8	27.1
9	28.3
10	29.6
11	30.9
12	32.1
13	33.4
14	34.6
15	35.9
16	37.2
17	38.4
18	39.7
19	40.9
20	42.2
21	43.4
22	44.7
23	46.0
24	47.2
25	48.5
26	50.0
27	51.0
28	52.3
29	53.5
30	54.8
31	56.1
32	57.3
33	58.6
34	59.9
35	61.1
36	62.4
37	63.6
38	64.9
39	66.2
40	67.4
41	68.7
42	69.9

Spousal Inventory of Desired Change and Relationship Barriers: SIDCARB

Factor III

Raw Score	Standard Score
4	38.3
5	40.0
6	41.6
7	43.3
8	45.0
9	46.6
10	48.3
11	50.0
12	51.6
13	53.3
14	55.0
15	56.6
16	58.3
17	60.0
18	61.6
19	63.3
20	65.0
21	66.6
22	68.3
23	70.0
24	71.6
25	73.3
26	75.0
27	76.6
28	78.3

APPENDIX B

Personal Sexual History

Date: _____

Name: _____ Date of Birth: _____

Address: _____ Place of Birth: _____

_____

_____

Telephone: _____

Email: _____

Family of Origin Information

Mother's name: _____ Age _____ Deceased _____

Father's name: _____ Age _____ Deceased _____

Siblings:

Name	Age	Marital Status

I. *Childhood*
1. What is your first memory?
2. What is your first sexual memory?
3. When were you first aware of being a sexual person?
4. At what age do you remember first having sexual feelings?
5. Were these feelings accompanied by any fantasies? If so, what were these fantasies?
6. Were these sexual feelings experienced in connection with any particular activities, events, situations, or people? If so, explain.
7. Do you remember your reactions to having these sexual feelings and thoughts? If so, what were they?
8. How old were you when you learned "where babies come from"?
9. How did you learn about "where babies come from"?
10. Do you recall how you reacted to this information?
11. At what age did you put all the information together (e.g., menstruation, erection, ejaculation, intercourse, conception, childbirth)?
12. Do you recall playing sex games as a child?
13. If so, with whom did you play these games?
14. How old were you and how old were your sex game playmates?
15. Describe, as best you can, the nature of these sex games.
16. How did you feel about playing these games?
17. Were you ever caught by any adults while you were playing these games?
18. If so, what were the adults' reactions?
19. Were you ever punished for playing sex games as a child? If so, what was the punishment?
20. When you were a child, did you ever have an opportunity to see animals involved in sexual activities (e.g., having intercourse, having their young, nursing)? If so, what was your reaction?
21. When you were a child, did you ever have the opportunity to see anyone else, accidentally or otherwise, involved in sexual activity?
22. If so, were they children or adults?
23. Did they know that you observed them?
24. If yes, what was their reaction?
25. Did you ever have an opportunity to observe your parents engaging in sexual intercourse or any other form of sexual activity? If yes, describe:
    (a) your reaction
    (b) your interpretation of what you observed
    (c) your feelings about your mother
    (d) your feelings about your father

II. *Adolescence and Adulthood*
     Females
     26. At what age did you begin to menstruate?
     27. What was your reaction to your first menstruation?
     28. How did you feel about menstruating during adolescence?
     29. Was menstruation factually explained to you well in advance of your first menstruation?
     30. If yes, by whom?
     31. Was the person who explained menstruation to you comfortable with this discussion?
     32. If no one prepared you for the onset of menstruation, how did you deal with getting your first period?
     33. How did you feel about it?
     34. Was the onset of menstruation considered by you to be something (a) positive, (b) negative, or (c) neutral?
     35. Have you ever had any menstrual difficulties?
     36. Do you consider yourself as experiencing PMS?
     37. Do any of the women in your family experience PMS?
     38. By what term or terms do you refer to menstruation?
     39. At what age did you start to notice your breasts beginning to develop?
     40. What was your reaction to your breasts beginning to develop?
     41. Were there any reactions to your breasts developing by parents or other family members that you can recall? If yes, what were these reactions?
     42. As a teenager, were you satisfied with how your breasts developed? Their shape? Their size?
     43. As a teenager, were you satisfied with how your body developed (hips, thighs, legs, etc.)?
     44. As a teenager, how did you feel about your overall physical appearance (face, body type, height, size, etc.)?
     45. Now, at this time in your life, how do you feel about your breasts, hips, thighs, legs, face, body type, height, and overall physical appearance?
     46. If you have had children, how do you feel about the changes in your body that have taken place?
     47. If you are currently going through menopause or if you have completed menopause, how has this process affected you and your feelings about yourself as a sexual person?

Males

48. How old were you when you began to notice changes in your genitals (e.g., penis development, testicular development, pubic hair)?
49. How did you react to these changes?
50. How did you feel about these changes?
51. At what age do you remember having spontaneous erections?
52. What was your reaction to them?
53. How did you feel about having erections?
54. How old were you when you had your first nocturnal emissions?
55. What was your reaction to them?
56. How did you feel about them?
57. Did anyone (parents, siblings, etc.) ever say anything to you about your nocturnal emissions? If yes, who was the person? What was his or her reaction?
58. Had the changes that were taking place in your body during puberty been explained to you beforehand by anyone? If yes, by whom?
59. Was the person who explained these changes to you comfortable with the discussion?
60. As a teenager, were you satisfied with how your penis and testicles developed (size, shape, etc.)?
61. As a teenager, were you satisfied with how your body developed?
62. As a teenager, how did you feel about your overall physical appearance (face, body type, height, size, etc.)?
63. Now, at this time in your life, how do you feel about your penis size, testicles, and overall physical appearance?

Males and Females

64. Have you ever had any cosmetic procedures performed in order to change aspects of your physical appearance? If yes:
    (a) How old were you at the time?
    (b) What changes were made?
    (c) Were you satisfied with the results?
    (d) How do you now feel about having made these changes?
    (e) Have you ever had any regrets about having made these changes?
    (f) How did people who knew about these changes respond to you? What were their reactions?
    (g) How did these changes in your physical appearance affect your sex life? Your life in general?

65. At what age did you first experiment with masturbation or with any kind of solitary activity that produced a genital feeling of pleasure?
66. How frequently did you engage in these activities?
67. With what frequency do you use masturbatory release now?
68. Do you have specific fantasies when you masturbate? If yes, describe the most common fantasies.
69. Have your fantasies changed in content over the years? If yes, how have they changed?
70. Do these fantasies differ in content from any fantasies you have during sexual intercourse? If yes, explain.
71. What are your feelings about masturbation?
72. At what age did you have your first sexual experience that involved another person?
73. How old was the other person?
74. Was this person of the same sex or the opposite sex?
75. What was the nature of this sexual activity?
76. How did you feel during the activity?
77. How did you feel after the activity?
78. For how long did these activities continue?
79. Why did they end?

III. *Early Dating and Sexual Experiences*
80. At what age did you begin to date?
81. In groups?
82. Single dating?
83. When did you begin to steady date?
84. What kind of sexual behavior did you engage in with your dating partners?
    (a) Kissing
    (b) Fondling/petting/genital manipulation
    (c) Masturbation
    (d) Oral sex
    (e) Anal sex
85. With all partners or just with selected individuals?
86. Did any of these behaviors ever lead to intercourse?
87. If so, describe your first experience with intercourse.
88. What was your reaction to your first experience with intercourse?
89. How did you feel during this first experience?
90. How did you feel after this first experience?
91. Was contraception used in this first experience?

92. If contraception was used, who accepted the responsibility for using contraception?
93. If contraception was not used during this first experience with sexual intercourse, did pregnancy result? If pregnancy did result, did you have the child or was the pregnancy terminated? How did you feel about your decision?
94. Subsequent to your first experience with sexual intercourse, did you use any means of contraception? If yes, explain.
95. Under what circumstances did sexual intercourse usually occur?
96. Were you ever raped or forced to perform sexual acts against your will?
97. If yes, describe the circumstances, consequences, and your feelings.
98. (For females) Did rape result in you becoming pregnant? If yes, did you have the child or terminate the pregnancy?
    (a) How did you feel then about the action you had taken?
    (b) Now, in retrospect, how do you feel about the action you had taken?
    (c) Have there been additional pregnancies which you chose to terminate? If yes, how do you feel about these decisions?
    (d) How have these experiences (rape, pregnancy, termination of pregnancy, etc.) affected your life and your sexual functioning?
99. (For males) Did you ever rape anyone or force someone to engage in sexual acts against his or her will?
    (a) If yes, describe the circumstances and the consequences.
    (b) How has this experience affected your life and your sexual functioning?
100. Have you ever contracted a sexually transmitted disease? If yes, explain.
101. Do you still have this condition?
102. If yes, what precautions do you take not to infect others?
103. If you have not had a sexually transmitted disease, what types of precautions do you use to avoid contracting a sexually transmitted disease?
103. As a teenager, were you ever caught and punished for your sexual behavior? If yes, explain.
105. Have you ever had homosexual experiences?
106. At what age did you have your first homosexual experience? Describe this experience.
107. How did you feel during this experience?
108. How did you feel after this experience?

109. How frequently during your adolescence and adult life have you engaged in homosexual activities?
110. Do you consider your sexual orientation to be primarily:
    (a) Heterosexual
    (b) Homosexual
    (c) Bisexual

IV. *Significant Relationships*
111. How old were you when you became involved in what you consider to be your first significant sexual relationship?
112. Was this sexual relationship considered by you to be satisfying and fulfilling?
113. Was this sexual relationship considered by your partner to be satisfying and fulfilling?
114. Since this first significant relationship ended, how many other significant sexual relationships have you had in your adult life (including marriages)?
115. Did any of these relationships/marriages end because of sexual problems or infidelities? If yes, explain.
116. During any of these previous relationships were you ever separated from your partner for long periods of time? If yes, how did you satisfy your sexual desires and need for sexual intimacy during these periods apart?
117. Currently, how do you satisfy your sexual desires and need for sexual intimacy when you and your partner are separated for long periods of time?

V. *Present Marriage/Relationship*
118. How long did you date your current partner before you had sexual intercourse with him or her?
119. How would you characterize your first experience of sexual intercourse with your current partner?
120. How did you feel during this experience?
121. How did you feel after this experience?
122. Do you experience your sexual relationship with your partner now to be satisfying and fulfilling? If no, explain.
123. Do you believe that your partner experiences his or her sexual relationship with you now to be satisfying and fulfilling? If no, explain.
124. Has the frequency of sexual intercourse with your partner changed considerably since you first began to have intercourse as a couple? If yes:
    (a) How do you account for this change?

       (b) How do you feel about this change?

       (c) If you are unhappy with this change, what have you done to correct the problem?

125. Have you experienced a change in your desire for sexual intercourse with your partner recently? If yes:

       (a) Has your desire and need increased?

       (b) Has your desire and need decreased?

       (c) To what do you attribute this change in desire and need?

126. How much, if any, extramarital/extra-relationship sexual activity has occurred on your part during this marriage/relationship?

127. How do you feel about your behavior?

128. In what ways has your extramarital/extra-relationship activities affected your relationship with your partner?

129. Does your partner know about these extramarital/extra-relationship activities?

130. If yes, what has been his or her reaction?

131. To your knowledge, has there been any extramarital/extra-relationship sexual activity on the part of your partner?

132. If yes, what has been your reaction?

133. How has this knowledge affected your relationship with your partner?

134. What were your expectations regarding sexual behavior and lovemaking prior to this marriage/relationship in terms of frequency and types of sexual activities in which you and your partner would engage?

135. Were these expectations met and fulfilled at some point within the first year of marriage/relationship?

136. If not, how did these unmet expectations affect your marriage/relationship?

137. How did you feel about these unmet expectations?

138. Have you and your partner discussed this issue?

139. If yes, what has been the outcome?

140. On a weekly basis, how frequently do you have sexual intercourse with your partner?

141. Are you satisfied with this frequency?

142. Is your partner satisfied with this frequency?

143. If there is some dissatisfaction on your part, or on your partner's part, what have you done to correct this problem?

144. What has had the most influence on when or how frequently or under what circumstances you and your partner have sexual intercourse?

145. Who usually chooses the time?
146. Who usually takes the initiative?
147. Are you satisfied with this situation? If no, explain.
148. Does sexual activity always lead to intercourse?
149. If yes, how do you feel about this situation?
150. Do you have a preference for a particular time of day or night for having intercourse?
151. Does your partner have a preference for a particular time of day or night for having intercourse?
152. Do you and your partner have different time of day preferences? If yes, has this caused a problem in your marriage/relationship?
153. Do you feel free to express your desire for intercourse and need for sexual intimacy to your partner at any time and anticipate a warm and receptive response? If no, explain.
154. Describe the kinds of situations that you find the most sexually stimulating and desirable.
155. Which situations do you find to be the least stimulating and desirable?
156. Do you openly communicate to your partner what pleases you sexually and what displeases you sexually?
157. What is his or her response to your open communication of your likes and dislikes?
158. Is your partner able to communicate his or her sexual desires and need for sexual intimacy to you openly and clearly?
159. What trait, behavioral pattern, habit, or characteristic does your partner have that tends to diminish your sexual attraction and desire for him or her?
160. What trait, behavioral pattern, habit, or characteristic do you have that you believe makes you sexually unattractive to your partner?
161. (For females) Does having your period affect your sexual desire and need for sexual intimacy? If yes, explain.
162. (For males) How does your partner's having her period affect your sexual desire for her and your need for sexual intimacy with her?
163. Do you still find your partner to be sexually attractive and desirable? If no, explain.
164. Do you still consider yourself to be sexually attractive and desirable to your partner? If no, explain.
165. What do you want most in the way of sexual attitudes, behaviors, activities, etc., from your partner that he or she does not provide to you now?

166. What sexual attitudes, behaviors, activities, etc., do you receive from your partner that you value most?
167. How satisfactory has the sexual component of your current marriage/relationship been when compared to previous sexual relationships?
168. Do you and your partner have a sense of humor, and is humor a part of your sexual relationship?

VI. *Family and Cultural Influences*
169. Were sex and sexual matters discussed openly in your family?
170. Were your parents comfortable discussing sexual material with each other? With you?
171. Were you allowed to ask questions about sex in your family?
172. Who was more receptive to such questions and discussions? Mother_____ Father_____ Siblings_____
173. Do you consider your father to be a sexual person?
174. Do you consider your mother to be a sexual person?
175. Which parent do you consider to be the more sexual?
176. As you were growing up, what were your childhood/adolescent impressions of your parents' sexual relationship?
177. What is your impression of your parents' current sexual relationship?
178. Do you think that your parents had any sexual problems in their marriage? If so, explain.
179. Was either parent ever unfaithful? If yes, explain.
180. Do you think difficulties in their sexual relationship contributed to the infidelity? If yes, explain.
181. In what religion were you raised?
182. Do you consider your parents to be religious people?
183. Do you consider your parents to be spiritual people?
184. Do you consider yourself to be a religious person?
185. Do you consider yourself to be a spiritual person?
186. In what ways have your religion and your religious beliefs affected your views, attitudes and feelings about sexual matters?
187. In what ways have your religion and your religious beliefs affected your sexual behavior and the sexual acts you will engage in?
188. If you and your partner have had children, how did the births of these children affect your sexual functioning as a couple?
189. Did the presence of children living in your home affect your sexual functioning as a couple? If yes, explain.

190. Describe any of the following factors that you believe have influenced your sexual attitudes, feelings, behaviors, expectations, etc.
    (a) Ethnic background
    (b) Race
    (c) National origin or ancestry
    (d) Regional or community mores, norms, and values
    (e) Socioeconomic status
    (f) Other

VIII. *Sexual Problem Section*
    191. Do you consider there to be a sexual problem in your current marriage/relationship?
    192. If yes, describe the problem in detail.
    193. What significance does the problem have with regard to your own sexual functioning?
    194. How do you think these problems affect your partner's sexual functioning?
    195. (If dysfunction is present in both partners) Which problem do you recall as having developed first?
    196. How have you, *personally*, handled the problem(s) to date?
    197. How have you and your partner tried to handle this problem in the past?
    198. What techniques have been helpful?
    199. What techniques have not been helpful?
    200. What is your concept of effective sexual functioning?
        (a) For yourself?
        (b) For your partner?
    201. (For females) Under what circumstances have you been orgasmic, if ever? Describe the feelings (physical) that you associate with the experience.
    202. (For males) Has your partner ever been orgasmic? Under what circumstances?
    203. (For male)s Have you ever had erectile or ejaculatory difficulties? If so, describe:
        (a) first occurrence
        (b) frequency
        (c) situation
        (d) global
        (e) specific

204. (For females) Have you ever noted erectile or ejaculatory difficulties on your partner's part? If so, describe.
205. By what means, other than intercourse, have you sought to bring sexual pleasure to your partner? Describe results.
    (a) Which techniques do you prefer and enjoy?
    (b) Which techniques do you dislike or avoid?
206. By what means has your partner attempted to bring sexual pleasure to you? Describe results.
    (a) Which techniques do you prefer and enjoy?
    (b) Which techniques do you dislike or avoid?
207. What is your concept of appropriate male and female roles in a sexual relationship?
208. How do you think your partner would answer this question?

APPENDIX C

Sexual Attitudes and Practices Questionnaire

Part I

1. What do you consider to be the most sexually attractive aspect of your partner's physical appearance? How do you think your partner would answer this question?
2. What do you consider to be the most sexually attractive aspect of your partner's personality? How do you think your partner would answer this question?
3. What do you consider to be the most sexually attractive aspect of your physical appearance? How do you think your partner would answer this question?
4. What do you consider to be the most sexually attractive aspect of your personality? How do you think your partner would answer this question?
5. Describe what you consider to be your ideal conditions and circumstances for having sexual intercourse with your partner. How do you think your partner would answer this question?
6. How frequently, on a weekly basis, would you like to have sexual intercourse with your partner? How do you think your partner would answer this question?
7. Do you enjoy engaging in sex play with your partner that does not always lead to intercourse or orgasm? How do you think your partner would answer this question?
8. What do you consider to be the most sexually exciting, stimulating, and erotic experiences that you have had with your partner? How do you think your partner would answer this question?

Part II

Listed below are some of the most common sexual practices that couples engage in together. For each of the practices listed, circle one of these four possible options:

(a) I have done this with my partner, and *I enjoy it.*
(b) I have done this with my partner but *I do not enjoy it.*
(c) I have not done this with my partner, but *I would like to try it.*
(d) I have not done this with my partner and *I would not like to try it.*

1. Watching my partner dress and undress	a	b	c	d
2. My partner watching me dress and undress	a	b	c	d
3. Seeing my partner naked	a	b	c	d
4. My partner seeing me naked	a	b	c	d
5. Giving my naked partner a body massage	a	b	c	d
6. My partner giving me a body massage while I'm naked	a	b	c	d
7. Caressing my partner's chest/breasts and buttocks	a	b	c	d
8. My partner caressing my chest/breasts and buttocks	a	b	c	d
9. Kissing, licking, sucking, etc., my partner's chest/breasts	a	b	c	d
10. My partner kissing, licking, sucking, etc., my chest/breasts	a	b	c	d
11. Caressing my partner's genitals	a	b	c	d
12. My partner caressing my genitals	a	b	c	d
13. Masturbating my partner	a	b	c	d
14. My partner masturbating me	a	b	c	d
15. Watching my partner masturbate	a	b	c	d
16. My partner watching me while I masturbate	a	b	c	d
17. Kissing, licking, sucking, etc., my partner's genitals	a	b	c	d
18. My partner kissing, licking, sucking, etc., my genitals	a	b	c	d
19. Bringing my partner to orgasm through oral stimulation	a	b	c	d
20. My partner bringing me to orgasm through oral stimulation	a	b	c	d
21. Having sexual intercourse with my partner	a	b	c	d
22. Having intercourse with my partner using various positions	a	b	c	d
23. Having anal intercourse with my partner	a	b	c	d

Are there any other sexual activities you would like to discuss with your partner that are not listed above? If yes, list them below:

APPENDIX D

Sensate Focus

☐ Nongenital Sensate Focus Experiments

Introduction

The goal of sensate focus is to allow increasingly pleasurable feelings to emerge for you and your partner. Sensate focus is designed to help you learn nondemand and non-goal-oriented touch. Through this nondemand touching you can rediscover the pleasure that touching and being touched by your partner can bring. Through this exercise, you can focus on what style of touching, stroking, petting, and caressing feels most enjoyable.

For the best results, you should do the sensate focus exercises *three times a week.* Since these exercises were developed to facilitate both physical pleasure and ease with asking and being asked for touch without a performance goal, *you should not engage in any form of sexual stimulation or sexual intercourse on the three days of the week that you plan to do these exercises.*

General Guidelines

These exercises are intended to increase awareness of choices and variations in physical sensations. As a couple, you can find out what feels good to you, what you like, and what you dislike in the way of touching and being touched by your partner. Use the communication skills you have learned to tell your partner what types of touch you enjoy. If your partner touches you in a way that you do not find to be pleasurable, ask him or her to change to a form of stroking, touching, and so forth, that you experience as pleasurable. You can guide your partner verbally or with your hands while making a request for change. Be very specific about what you want.

These exercises should not be rushed. You should only plan to do them when you have ample time. Make sure that there will be no interruptions or distractions during these exercises.

Showering before beginning these exercises is recommended. You may shower or bathe together, but remember that there should be no genital touching or sexual fondling during bathing or drying your partner. After bathing or showering, proceed to the bedroom nude or with a towel wrapped around you if nakedness is uncomfortable for you. The bedroom should be comfortably warm. The amount of light needed for these exercises is a matter of individual taste. You and your partner should agree upon how well lit or how dimly lit your bedroom should be during these exercises. Sensate focus should be done unclothed. If being totally naked is not comfortable for you, you should begin by wearing as little as possible, but eventually these exercises should be done naked.

Reciprocity and Receptivity are central to all forms of intimacy. Therefore, each partner is expected to be both giver of pleasure and receiver of pleasure during sensate focus. You are to take turns, either during the same session or on different days. Each partner must have the opportunity to be both giver and receiver. Guidelines for the *Receiver* of pleasure and the *Giver* of pleasure are listed below:

Receiver Guidelines

1. Be passive and only receive pleasure. Do not touch, stroke, pet, etc., the giver. Only focus on being touched.
2. Speak only to give your partner feedback about what you like or what you would like him or her to change.
3. For the first exercise, keep your eyes closed. Focus on your own bodily sensations.
4. Be aware of your entire body being touched. Experience what types of touch are comfortable, relaxing, soothing, sensuous, sexual, or arousing. Don't act on any sexual impulses if you become sexually aroused. Just make a mental note of it and keep it to yourself, for now.
5. Tell your partner how you like, and don't like, to be touched. Do this in a way that is informative and not critical. Frequently, partners touch each other during sensate focus in ways that they themselves like to be touched. Therefore, your partner may be touching you in a way that he or she finds pleasurable. If you do not enjoy being touched this way, request a change, but ask your partner if he or she would like to be touched that way by you when it is your turn to be the giver.
6. Sometimes being touched in a particular way or being touched on a certain place on your body may produce aversive feelings or evoke unpleasant memories. If this occurs, make a mental note to talk to your partner about it later.

Giver Guidelines

1. Approach your partner as someone wonderful to look at, touch, and be with. Do not talk to your partner. Only speak to your partner in response to his or her requests. Allow your partner the silence to focus upon his or her own feelings.
2. Trust your partner to tell you how to touch or how to change your touch. Do not ask for feedback. Your partner will give it to you as needed.
3. Hear your partner's request for touching as information only, not as a criticism of you or what you are doing.
4. Focus on your own hands and whatever other part of your body you are using to bring pleasure to your partner (remember, do not touch your partner with your genitals or touch your partner's genitals). Note how your partner's skin feels on your hands, where it is smooth, rough, hairy, fuzzy, bumpy, velvety, curvy, cool, warm, etc.
5. If you feel uncomfortable with any of your partner's requests, tell your partner. If you feel tired, take a break. Take responsibility for your own comfort so that your partner does not feel responsible for your comfort. Your partner's responsibility is to focus on his or her own comfort.

Session I

The receiver should begin by lying face down. The giver should begin by gently massaging the receiver's shoulders using his or her hands and moving slowly up and down the receiver's back and sides. The giver then moves slowly to the receiver's waist and gently massages the receiver's spine with his or her thumbs, gently pressing and kneading this area and the lower back.

Next the giver should move up the receiver's back to his or her neck and head so that a scalp massage can be given. When this has been done, the giver can again return to the receiver's back.

Next, the giver moves to the receiver's arms, hands, legs, and feet, gently massaging these limbs until the backs of both arms, legs, and feet have been massaged.

Finally, the giver massages the receiver's buttocks and thighs. The intent here is to give the receiver pleasure—not to sexually stimulate the receiver. When the giver is finished, it is the receiver's turn. The receiver and giver then switch roles.

Session II

This time, the partner who was last the receiver takes the role of giver. The receiver once again lies on his or her stomach and experiences being touched—this time with his or her eyes open. In this second session the receiver guides the giver's hands to certain parts of his or her body. Verbal prompts can be used if necessary. The receiver should guide the giver to those parts of his or her body that are particularly sensuous. At this time, the giver can kiss, lick, or use his or her hair to stimulate the partner's back. Gentle love bites also are permitted.

When the receiver is ready, he or she should turn over onto his or her back. The receiver then closes his or her eyes and assumes a passive, relaxed attitude. The giver caresses the receiver's hands, fingertips, palms, forearms, and arms. Next the giver moves to the face, forehead, cheeks, nose, lips, and chin. Kissing the receiver's closed eyes is also something that the giver might do. The giver should avoid touching the breasts and nipples and proceed to the stomach and sides. Next, the giver moves to the thighs and legs, again avoiding the genital area. If the receiver becomes sexually aroused, he or she should not act on these sexual impulses. It is fine if there is no sexual arousal, as the exercise is designed to help you explore and learn. Sexual arousal is not the goal.

Next the giver touches the fronts of the legs and feet of the receiver. When this is done, the partners should switch roles.

Session III

For this session, the partners are requested to use body lotion. This is a less structured session. Partners now engage in a mutual give and take. The structured roles of giver and receiver should be discontinued. The emphasis in this exercise is on the partners guiding each other, teaching each other what feels good and sensuous on the front of the body. Partners are asked to keep their eyes open and make appropriate eye contact. Each partner should guide his or her partner's hands, showing the partner nonverbally how and where he or she likes to be touched. The partners can now experiment with full body contact, holding, hugging and caressing freely and spontaneously. As the exercise progresses, the partners may wish to talk to each other, making requests for certain types of touch, and expressing their feelings about what they are experiencing. Partners should feel free to give each other compliments and comment upon the pleasure they are experiencing. This exercise should end with the partners holding each other, cuddling face-to-face or back-to-front (spoon style).

INDEX

Index note: page references in italics indicate a chart or figure.